The Great

P.K.
the Great

Colleen L. Reece

Review and Herald® Publishing Association
Washington, DC 20039-0555
Hagerstown, MD 21740

This book was
Edited by Richard W. Coffen
Designed by Bill Kirstein
Cover art by Jackie Magee
Type set: Times Roman 10/12

PRINTED IN U.S.A.

94 93 92 91 90   10 9 8 7 6 5 4 3 2 1

R&H Cataloging Service

Reece, Colleen Loraine, 1935-
P.K. the great.
        I. Title.

ISBN 0-8280-0560-5

Contents

Jack's Letter
to God

Hey, Jack!'' Felicity Nelson burst into her year-older brother's room. ''Hurry it up. Mom's waiting to take us to the youth meeting.'' She stopped short and stared at the figure hunched over the corner desk. The dark eyes that matched her shining hair opened wide. ''Don't tell me you haven't done your assignment yet.''

''Get outa here, will you?'' Jack's red-setter hair waved wildly from running his fingers through it. ''I'm almost done.'' He quickly wrote a few more words and ignored his sister's impatient, ''If you'd do what you're supposed to right away instead of waiting until the last minute . . .'' The rest of the familiar sermon slid over Jack's ignoring ears.

''There.'' Jack triumphantly folded the single page, pushed past Felicity, tore down the hall and shouted back, ''Come *on*, Flis. Why do you always have to take so long?''

She ran after him in hot pursuit but Jack had already dodged out the kitchen door and climbed into the front seat—next to Mom—of the Toyota. He grinned like a demon.

''So what's on for your meeting tonight?'' Mom wanted to know. Her smiling dark eyes reflected her daughter's features exactly. So did her short dark hair and tall slender figure. Shirley Nelson always amazed friends when they discovered she was mother to a 14-year-old and a 13-year-old.

"Tim asked us each to write a letter to God," Felicity promptly answered.

Jack scowled. *He'd* been going to tell Mom. Why did Flis have to get ahead of him? He twisted his neck and caught the excitement in her eyes, then smiled to himself. If she only knew what he'd put in his letter, she'd look a lot different. For a moment he seriously considered shocking the socks off her by letting her read his assignment. The next instant he decided against it. Tim had said no one had to share a letter at the meeting except those who wanted to. Well, there was no way he'd read his out loud!

Jack turned and stared out the window, vaguely seeing the familiar Vancouver, Washington, streets, the early Christmas decorations, the late November rain and ground fog. They faded as he let himself picture what a bombshell that one crumpled page in his pocket could be if he read it. He could see the smile die from their leader Tim's usually happy face; the way the other kids would laugh or look away or stare; Felicity's face turn scarlet with anger and embarrassment. Most of all he could hear himself saying, "Tim said we could write anything we wanted to God. Well, here's what I wrote:

Dear God,

   Everyone says You never make mistakes. I'm not so sure about that. If it's true, how come You made me the way I am? It's bad enough to look just like my dog Dusty, except he doesn't have freckles and I have trillions of them. Red hair curlier than the spiral in my notebook. Red-brown eyes enough like Dusty's that if he wasn't a dog, people would think we were twins.

   If You had to color me weird, how come You also made me *short?* Fourteen years old and 5 foot 4? Who are You kidding? I used to wonder if I even belonged to the Nelson family. Dad, Mom, and Flis are so dark, but I'm the family stoplight. I know I do belong, though. Grandpa Nelson's another red setter person—except he's tall, as tall as Dad.

Being a P.K. isn't all that much fun, either. Don't get me wrong, God. I'm proud that Dad chose to be a minister, but I wish everyone at church would get over the idea that P.K. means Perfect Kid. Every time I even think about doing something unusual, someone gives me the 140th version of the 'you-need-to-set-a-good-example-for-the-other-kids-so-they-can-see-that-what-your-father-preaches-is-for-real' guilt trip.

Yeah, I know, God, it's not so bad at school. There are some other P.K.'s at academy, even in my 9th grade class. I'm not the Lone Ranger, or anything like that. But none of *them* are speckled and short. Just me. I'll bet I'm even shorter than Zacchaeus. There aren't any sycamores around, but if You came walking down Main Street I'd have to climb on top of one of the stores to see You.

The worst thing is, almost every boy I know has grown taller this year. Me? Not a bit. Dad told me about a kid who went to school when he did who was really shrimpy—all the way through to graduation. Then he went away into the service. When he came back he was about six feet tall! Maybe they gave him tall pills, or something. I'm too young to go in the service but do You suppose You could make me grow, or something? I don't want to spend the rest of my life as a zero. I can't change being a P.K. I guess I don't even really want to. But it would sure be nice to be P.K. the Great. . . .

"How about getting back to the real world and getting out?" Felicity's question jerked Jack to reality. He resisted the urge to stick his tongue out at her, even when she rolled her eyes and drew circles in the air by her head. Misery filled him. First, God had made him short and doggy-colored, then sent a really beautiful sister like Flis along. He watched her glow her way into the meeting room, torn between being proud that she was so well-liked and pretty and wishing things came as easily for him. They both pulled top grades, but he had to study hard for them; Flis barely cracked a book. And when an election came along, he stuck his nose in the air and said, "Not me.

I'm too busy,'' knowing that he'd have to beat people over the head to get enough votes to be elected. All Flis had to do was smile, and you guessed it—Madam President all over the place.

"Well, how did the letters go?" Tim Chiles had a not-so-secret way of being a great youth leader, and it came from his sincere desire to help kids find Christ as a personal friend and Saviour. He actually loved kids and often grinned and said, "What's 17-year-old me doing in this 27-year-old body?" Now his gray eyes danced with fun. "Anyone brave enough to read a letter to God?"

Jack scrunched down in his seat. That red-hot letter all wadded up in his pocket was going to stay right there. He'd been dumb to even write it, anyway. It sounded more like a whining 4-year-old than a teenager's letter.

A couple of the kids read their letters. The usual stuff, about how glad they were they knew God, how thankful they felt with Christmas coming up and a time to remember God's great gift of His Son. Hot and cold at the thought of his earlier delight in how he could explode the meeting with *his* letter, Jack wiggled out of his jacket.

Some Christian you are, a little voice whispered inside. *Not one word did you write to God except how disgusted you are with yourself. How come you couldn't at least say thanks for a neat home and family?*

Jack glanced around and heaved a sigh of relief. No one was looking at him. For a split second he'd felt all twenty-some people in the room had the ability to read through his pocket. Twenty-some people meant forty-some eyes. Gray, brown, blue, green, looking, accusing.

By the time Flis stood to read her letter, as Jack knew she would, he'd about had it. The last thing he needed was to hear what his sister had to say. He pushed in front of a couple of kids and headed for the door, not even excusing himself. Once through it he paused, making sure the door stayed open enough so he could hear, welcoming the cold air sneaking in around the corner of the hall.

The pink sweater Flis had on matched the color of her cheeks. He knew without seeing because he could remember the way she looked earlier. Her soft, clear voice floated to him, and again Jack felt the same war between pride and resentment that had started a couple years ago. Funny. Until he was almost 13 he hadn't felt this way. Sure, they argued, mostly about the table games they played, because Jack couldn't stand losing, but a lot of the time they enjoyed doing things together. As P.K.'s they'd moved now and then, and just knowing that Flis felt the same way he did about having to make new friends and stuff kept them close.

Then suddenly Flis became his rival. Maybe in his own mind. Or was it? From where he stood, it sure looked like Dad and Mom thought Flis was a perfect 10. What did they think he was? A 5? A 2? Maybe a minus 1? He didn't want to know. He had enough troubles without that. Yeah, they loved him, but how could they be proud of a kid who wasn't tall enough for basketball, heavy enough for football, popular enough to be accepted as he was, and too scared to even offer a table blessing unless it was just for their family?

I'm going to do something to make them proud, he resolved. *Something big and great and something Flis can't ever do.* Even as he made his vow, he knew he was being unfair to his parents and Flis. From the time he had been old enough to scribble pictures for the fridge Dad and Mom had praised him. So had Flis. They still did. Look how they raved when he got that dumb story posted on the bulletin board at school.

Jack had lost the beginning of Felicity's letter in his daydreaming. Now he heard her say, "So, God, what I really want this Christmas is answers. When I talk to kids who don't know You, and who ask me stuff like why You let terrible earthquakes and wars happen and why little kids get killed in accidents, I need to know what to tell them. Maybe what I really want is the determination to study the Scriptures, 'cause I know the answers are in there."

Jack stood tensely. Something in his sister's voice really got to him. She finished by saying, "Someday You'll return, and there'll be peace, and no one will be hungry or cold or hurting. Please, let me always remember that and do what I can to help make others accept You so they'll be ready, too."

Jack bit his lip until it ached. Disgust with himself gnawed away inside. No wonder people loved Flis. She deserved it. Imagine, a

13-year-old kid into heavy stuff like that while he sat around feeling sorry for himself!

His mood lasted through the rest of the meeting, affecting the way he acted. One of the kids commented, "What's wrong, Jack? Are you sick? You haven't ordered anyone around since you got here."

"Lay off, will you?" Jack's automatic response shattered the mental groping he'd been doing ever since the serious part of the meeting ended. He spent the rest of the time alone in one corner, wishing he were anywhere but right there. What was the use? Even if he tried, he probably couldn't be anything except what he was.

It seemed hours before Mom appeared and the meeting ended. Felicity beat him to the car and grabbed the front seat. Part of him smirked, *See, she isn't so perfect,* but he silently got into the back seat and stared out the window all the way home.

Was it the way he failed after really trying to stop being so loud and having no one notice that made Jack so depressed the next couple of weeks? Seeing himself as the kids at the academy were used to seeing him told Jack why they treated him the same as always. If he made a suggestion, eyes rolled and patient expressions of, "It's just Jack. Ignore him and maybe he'll go away," settled on his classmates' faces. Once he stopped one of the popular kids and demanded, "What's with everyone? They act like I just got in from Mars, or somewhere."

The boy didn't even grin, just said, "Well, didn't you?" then howled at his joke and hurried on to class, leaving Jack standing there furious that he'd left himself wide open. After that, Jack gave it up. He argued with whatever the class discussed, getting bitter satisfaction out of knowing that if he couldn't be popular, at least he could speak out.

If Dad and Mom noticed Jack's struggles, they said nothing. But then with Christmas near, life took on hectic proportions. Dad accepted even more responsibility for some special work in Portland, organizing different groups to help collect money and food for unfortunate and homeless people. He didn't have to, but Jack knew that Dad intensely believed and lived by a little rhyme from a plaque in the Nelson's sunny kitchen:

"ONLY ONE LIFE, 'TWILL SOON BE PAST.
ONLY WHAT'S DONE FOR CHRIST WILL LAST."

Dad often said, "I have no idea who wrote it, but I'd like to shake the author's hand. It says it all."

The closer Christmas came, the busier things got. Even Jack lost some of his irritation with almost everything. He loved Christmas, always had. Decorations grew all over the three-bedroom ranch-style Nelson house, and when one mid-December morning they awakened to the first snow of the season, the purity of the world outside brought welcome peace. How could anyone stay mad when hills invited and soon turned into a din of flying sleds? One big field not far from the Nelsons' home sloped gently, then sharply, then flattened out for a long coast. Jack and Flis bundled up, forgot to put each other down, and spent most of the day in the snow with neighbor friends.

Blue dusk caught them and they walked home slowly, reluctant to let the day end and to see their friends dropping off at their homes.

"Know what I like?" Flis asked, patting snow between her mittens after the last friend had cheerfully called, "Good night" and had run into her home.

"What?" Jack stuck his tongue out and caught snowflakes the way he'd done when he was a kid. No one could see what he was doing, not even Flis.

"Lights in windows." She waved at the line of ranch style homes ahead. "It's like they're saying welcome."

"Talking lights?" Jack dodged the snowball she threw. Then unwilling to break the special evening he said, "Do you ever wish you were a little kid again?" and waited for her answer, half sorry that he'd asked.

"Yeah. A lot. It's not easy having to decide stuff for yourself. Dad and Mom always decided for us when we were little."

Jack relaxed. A desperate longing to be either younger or older filled him. And who would have thought Flis felt that way? Some of the joy they'd shared as kids seeped into his cold body, warming it better than even the blazing fire he knew Dad would have waiting in the fireplace.

"I wish—"

But Jack didn't get to find out what lay behind Felicity's wistful voice. Mom had opened the door and called, "Is that you, kids? You must be half frozen!" She stuck her head out the door. "Oh, it's snowing again. Neat." A wave of lasagna-warm-gingerbread perfume smothered them, and the chance to share anything else with Flis fled.

Sometime during the night Jack heard a hoarse cough. First he burrowed deeper under his covers. Wow, it must have turned freezing! He slept with his window open at least a crack year-round. Now it felt like a stream of ice water was pouring through it.

The cough came again, then Mom's low voice. Jack crawled out of bed and stepped into the hall. The door across the hall remained closed, so Flis couldn't have heard anything. But Mom and Dad's bedroom door stood open and light shone into the hall. Jack could see Mom getting into a quilted robe and shoving her feet into warm slippers. The next moment she came out. "Oh, Jack. What are you doing out here barefooted?"

Jack noticed the unaccustomed frown she wore. "Is Dad sick?"

"Yes." The flat word hung in the icy air and sent a matching chill through Jack. "I don't like the sound of that cough." Mom headed for the bathroom and Jack followed her. He watched her rummage through the medicine cabinet, take down Vicks VapoRub, the hot water bottle, and cough syrup. "I just hope this isn't the beginning of a virus," Mom muttered, running hot tap water into the bottle. "Dad's been really pushing it the past few weeks, and he never did get enough rest after he had that bad bronchitis last year."

"You're really worried, aren't you?" Jack hugged his mother. "Come on, Mom. Dad's strong. Besides, God won't let anything happen. He needs Dad too much." *So do we,* his heart added.

"Thanks, pal. I don't know what I'd do without you." Some of the anxiety left Mom's face. "Now get yourself back to bed before I have a second patient!"

Jack shivered his way into his room and dove back under his mountain of covers. Even his icy cold feet couldn't quite cool the happy warmth of Mom's words. "Anyone who can make Mom feel she can't get along without him can't be all bad," he mumbled into his pillow. But it took a long time for him to fall asleep again. And when

14

he did, it was with the prayer on his lips and in his heart: "Please, God, make what I said right. Don't let anything happen to Dad."

Several times during the rest of the night Jack slipped from bed and checked for light in his parents' room. There was none. Each time, he would pray before he went back to sleep, only to toss and turn, then restlessly get up and check again. If Mom needed him, he had to be there for her.

The last time Jack got up and checked his illuminated digital clock, it was 3 o'clock. Exhausted from all the exercise, fresh air, and fitful sleep, he fell into a deep and dreamless state.

Suddenly he found himself sitting straight up in bed. Foggy, still half asleep, he listened and heard the dreaded sound he knew must have awakened him, tearing coughing muffled by his closed door. Jack flew out of bed and to his parents' room. Dad had to be a lot worse to make that kind of noise.

CHAPTER
2

The Emergency Room

n his rush to check on Dad, Jack almost knocked Felicity down. Wide-eyed and scared, dark hair tumbling over her flannel gown, she clutched Jack's arm. "Wh—what's wrong?"

"Dad's sick." He saw her face whiten and knew he must look the same way. "Get something warm on before we have a second patient." Mom's words automatically came out of his mouth.

"You, too," she reminded, but first Jack had to know how Dad was. His mouth dropped when Mom met him at the door. He could see Dad sitting up, coughing, coughing, trying to get his breath. An unhealthy flush colored his face, and fever dimmed his usually sparkling dark eyes.

"Call the hospital Emergency Room and tell them we're bringing Dad in," Mom quietly told Jack. "His temperature is almost 104." She was back helping steady Dad almost before she finished speaking.

Jack ran down the hall, across the dining room, and jerked open the drawer in the table under the big window. His cold fingers almost dropped the phone book. Quickly he located the hospital number and dialed. A crisp voice answered on the second ring. "Vancouver Memorial, Emergency."

"This is Jack Nelson. We're bringing my dad in. He has a

temperature of almost 104 and can't stop coughing. . . . Yes, he's
having an awful time breathing. . . . No, we don't need an ambulance.
We're just a few minutes away.''

He hung up, tore back down the hall, glanced in at Dad, who still
coughed and leaned on Mom, then headed for his own room, ignoring
the cold, polished floorboards. By the time he had thrown on Levis,
heavy socks, and Reeboks, Felicity was calling, ''Ready?''

''Yeah.'' He shrugged into a heavy jacket and jerked open the
door.

''Mom and I bundled Dad up.'' Flis looked so small and scared
that Jack wanted to hug her but there wasn't time.

''Start the car, Jack,'' Mom said. ''Then come back and help me
with Dad. He's delirious enough that he won't be able to walk without
staggering.''

Never had the hall, dining room, and kitchen seemed miles long
until tonight. Jack stepped into a North Pole night, flicked the garage
door opener, and climbed into the Toyota. The engine was so cold it
turned over slowly but finally caught. Jack made sure it would keep
running then headed back down the hall. Mom and Flis hadn't tried to
get Dad dressed, just wrapped him in two bathrobes and a heavy quilt.
In spite of his fear, Jack noticed that one of them had grabbed two
different kinds of slippers.

''Make sure the door's locked behind us,'' Jack told Flis. Dad's
tall frame almost hung over Jack and Mom's shoulders and for about
the millionth time Jack wished he were taller. They got Dad into the
passenger's seat and tucked a second quilt over him. Mom slid behind
the wheel. Jack and Flis slid into the back seat.

''Seat belts?'' Mom's automatic question as she backed out then
closed the garage with the remote calmed her family by its very
usualness.

''Yeah.''

''Yes.''

''Take it easy, Mom.'' Jack rubbed frost from the car window and
checked outside. The snow had stopped. A lopsided moon grinned
down at them. Deep shadows from enormous cedars, fir, and pines

made crouching figures on the unbroken white. No wonder he'd felt the cold earlier.

"I will." Mom's competent gloved hands on the steering wheel expertly brought the little car out of a slide toward the edge of the road. Flis put her hand over her mouth but didn't cry out. Jack breathed easier, but he could feel his fingernails bite into the palms of his sweaty hands.

A male nurse met them at the emergency room door. He quickly helped transfer Dad to a gurney, nodding when Mom told him, "We've got a mighty sick man here." Over-sized doors opened and swallowed up the little procession. Jack had never been in an emergency room before. Neither had Flis. When the attendant beckoned Mom to follow him but waved the teenagers back, they stared at each other and moved to empty chairs nearby.

"Jack." His sister's voice cracked. "Do people die from pneumonia? Mom said she was pretty sure Dad has it."

"I don't think so. You know, penicillin and all that stuff they've got now." Jack tried to remember if he'd ever learned much about pneumonia. "Besides, maybe it isn't pneumonia. Maybe it's bronchitis again." He fell silent, knowing Flis was remembering the same way he did—how Dad had coughed almost endlessly, even with antibiotics.

"He's been working too hard." The prettiness in Felicity's face changed to anger. "Any time someone wants something done, it has to be Dad. He gets dumped on just because he's so good and willing to help."

Jack saw how quickly she turned away and knew Flis had started crying. He knew how she felt, too. Even though Dad always tried to laugh it off and said, "The way to get something done is to ask the busiest person around to do it," it wasn't fair. After all, God had said people were supposed to be His servants in helping others, not their slaves. Yet Dad couldn't live any other way, Jack suddenly knew. A ray of familiar pride mingled with his fear and anger. If ever he could be like Dad . . .

Once the initial shock of the wild events wore off a little, Jack looked around. The wall clock hands pointed to 5. Had the clock

18

stopped? It felt like they'd been sitting there forever. Flis drooped in her chair, eyes closed. She might be asleep. Maybe she was praying. Even though his brain had gone numb a long time ago, Jack became aware of a kind of chant chasing itself around inside him. A "please-God-make-Dad-OK," silent prayer.

A little stir in the corridor brought Jack to his feet and Flis straight in her chair. Maybe Mom had news. Instead, the same man who had brought Dad in rounded the corner with a gurney. The doors swung open. Moments later, a blanket-covered figure slid past. Jack heard Flis gasp. He tried to turn away from the shrouded mound, but when his straining ears caught the low words, "Heart; probably won't make it," he knew he had to get away. Like a homing pigeon he headed for the men's room down the hall, determined not to be sick. Seeing his own Kermit-the-Frog-colored face in the mirror, Jack threw cold water in his face. Wiping it roughly helped, and before he went back to Flis, he drank at the hall fountain until the ice water cooled him down.

Flis must not have heard what was said, for she still sat staring around the spotlessly scrubbed waiting room. Good. No need for her to have to stand anything else. Jack went back and sat down, then decided he had to do something. Anything.

"Uh," he cleared his throat and waited for the lady in the white pantsuit to look up. "Do you know anything about our Dad?"

How could a person who worked in a place like this smile? Jack wondered, but it did help some. And when she said, "Let me go check for you," Jack decided she had to be a Christian. Why else would she choose nursing, especially here?

The waiting ended soon. Mom came back with the nurse. Dark circles made her eyes even darker, but her smile lifted the ropes of fear that had been choking Jack. "He's going to be OK. He's in an oxygen tent, and they're getting all kinds of medication started."

"Can we see him?" Flis wanted to know.

"Not now. They've admitted him and want him to have complete rest." A little frown erased Mom's smile. "The doctor says he's really run down. You know Dad, he just keeps going, no matter what."

"Yeah." Jack felt another surge of resentment, but quickly hid it from Mom. She didn't need any more than she already had to worry about. "When can we see him?"

"Maybe this afternoon. I'll take you home and then come back. If it's OK for you to come later, I'll call and let you know when I'm coming after you."

A thousand protests rose in Jack. He even opened his mouth to say that he wanted to stay right at the hospital until he got to see Dad, then decided against it. Flis looked done in. She couldn't sit around a hospital waiting room, and neither should he. It would just worry Mom, for one thing. Besides, maybe there were things they could do at home to help. If Mom stayed most of the day at the hospital with Dad, someone had to be at home to make meals so she'd have something hot when she did return. Flis cooked great, but even their cozy home would get lonesome if she stayed alone.

"What can we do to help?" Flis must have caught his idea.

"Well," Mom said as she herded them out to the car, "someone's going to have to call people—Grandpa and Grandma Nelson, the assistant pastor, and Dad's substitute for the new Portland project. She stopped until they were all in the car and headed toward home. The roads had improved since their early morning trip. Road crews had obviously been out sanding.

"It would also be a good thing if you'd cook up some things that we can freeze. Frankly, even though the doctor says Dad will get better, I think we're in for a hard time ahead. If we have food prepared, then it will be easy to toss a salad and fix a hot vegetable to go with something from the freezer."

"Sure, Mom." Felicity hugged her mother as they got out and unlocked the kitchen door. "You can depend on us."

"I'll call first, then help Flis," Jack promised. For a minute he was tempted to ask Flis to make the call to Grandpa and Grandma but pushed it down. Just because he and Grandpa were so much alike that they didn't always get along very well was no reason to back off from doing what had to be done. By midafternoon they had accomplished a lot. All the phone calls had neat checkmarks next to them along with any messages Mom needed to know. Several hot dishes cooled on the garage shelf before getting put into the freezer, although as Flis said,

"I don't know why we bothered to cook." She giggled and Jack had to join in when she pointed to the kitchen counter. Three pies, two cakes, six casseroles, and a pan of cinnamon buns covered every inch of space. "Boy, you let people know someone's sick and they rush to the kitchen and start cooking and baking, I guess!"

It felt good to laugh. But after everything had been put away except the pot of spaghetti sauce simmering on the back burner getting ready for supper if or when Mom came, the echoes of their laughter died. Jack twined his fingers in Dusty's fur. Why didn't the phone ring? Mom should have called by now unless Dad had grown worse. Should he call the hospital? He shook his head. Mom would call when she could. Until then, all they could do was wait.

"I never knew animals were so sensitive to what goes on," Flis commented after a long, heavy silence. Firelight from the warm blaze Jack had kindled in the fireplace made little red flames in her dark hair. "Dusty has been restless all day. And Felix!" She pointed to the misnamed orange and white cat that looked nothing like the cartoon Felix. "Have you been watching him?"

"Yeah. It's kinda sad." Even as Jack spoke, the big cat that had come to them as a tiny, blue-eyed kitten uncurled himself from the hearth, marched down the hall, and scratched at the door of Dad's study. When the door remained closed, Felix cried and cried before coming back to the big living room.

"I guess he just doesn't understand how come Dad isn't here. He's so used to curling up on Dad's lap." A shine in her eyes betrayed Felicity's struggle to keep back fresh tears.

"Well, I don't curl up on Dad's lap anymore, but I don't like Dad not being here any more than Felix does!" Jack tried to laugh and was rewarded by an answering smile on his sister's lips.

The sharp ring of the phone brought them both to the dining room. Felicity held back, eyes wide, waiting for Jack to answer.

"Hello, Mom? What's happening?" Jack tried to sound calm, but his heart felt like it had permanently parked somewhere just behind his tonsils. "Yeah . . ." He covered the mouthpiece. "She's on her way home." Then, "OK." He hung up.

"Well?" Flis demanded.

21

"We can see him but just for a few minutes. They've brought the temperature down some, but it's just going to take time. Anyway, as soon as we eat we get to go back with her. I'll put the spaghetti on. The table's set."

Felicity followed him to the kitchen, talking as she worked. "I'll slip in some of the cinnamon rolls. I made a layered green salad earlier. With the spaghetti, that's enough."

Mom's face brightened at the sight and smell of the warm, attractive kitchen when she came in. "Great! All the way home I wished I'd told you earlier to do spaghetti. Where'd the rolls come from?"

"Church friends, along with a bunch of other stuff," Jack said. "What about Dad?"

Mom took off her heavy boots, coat, and mittens. Strength and peace radiated from her, warming their home and hearts. "It'll take time. Dad needs rest—lots of it. It's too soon to know just when he can come home, and of course we don' t want him to come until the doctor says it's OK. I don't know exactly what's ahead for us, but I do know that God has been good in the way your father's responding to treatment. Two of our elders came this afternoon and prayed for him. I know those prayers—and ours—are being answered."

Jack had to bite his tongue to keep from blurting out, "How come God let Dad get so sick in the first place?" Instead, he drained the spaghetti and set it on the table.

Mom asked the blessing, then helped herself. Some of the tiredness left her face after the good hot food gave her new body fuel. Jack suddenly realized he was starved, and Flis wasn't far behind. They'd just picked at their food for lunch.

A couple of hours later they were all back home. Jack and Flis had only been allowed to peek in at Dad. It seemed weird to see him so quiet in his hospital bed instead of up and around and busy. Jack was almost glad that Dad didn't open his eyes. The doctor had left word that Dad was doing "as well as could be expected"—whatever that was supposed to mean. Jack suspected the hospital said it to all the anxious people he saw in the halls and waiting rooms. Still, Dad looked a whole lot better than he had when he'd come to the hospital.

"We need to talk," Mom said. "First, even though it's early, let's get showered and into P.J.s and robes. Who wants first shower?"

"You do," Jack ordered.

"I won't argue with that. I feel like I've worn these clothes for a week." Mom laughed, a real laugh, not the sort of pretend one Jack and Flis had been using to keep up their spirits. Flis made warm cocoa. Jack popped some corn. Soon they gathered around the fireplace again. This time Felix seemed a little more content, but before long, he leaped from Mom's lap, took his walk down the hall to Dad's study, and went through his crying routine again.

When Jack saw Mom's wet eyes he said, "Dumb cat. He's been doing that all day," but he knew that neither Mom nor Flis thought he really meant Felix was dumb.

Mom hit the heart of the problem direct, the way she always did. "OK you two. I know right about now the biggest thing you're feeling is *why*. Right?"

This time Jack didn't bite his tongue fast enough. "You guessed it. Here Dad's knocking himself out for God, and God lets him get sick. I just don't get it."

Mom leaned forward. Jack had never seen her so serious. "Jack, Flis," she said as she reached one hand out to each of them. "God may have allowed Dad to get sick to slow down the terrific pace and strain he's been under before something worse happened."

Jack thought of the blanketed mound on the gurney and shivered. "Like a heart attack?"

"Maybe." Mom's gaze never wavered. "God expects us to use wisdom and to exercise good stewardship over our whole life, and that means over the way we serve Him, too. It isn't God's fault that your father extends himself too far because he desperately wants to witness and help others. It's our own responsibility to take good care of our health, to work *with* God in staying strong."

"Wow!" Wheels ground in Jack's head. "Then just maybe the bronchitis last year happened as a warning?"

"No one knows that." Mom's eyes looked almost black from her intensity. "We do know that now Dad has a real problem—and it's going to be up to us to do everything we can to face up to it. More importantly, to help Dad accept the fact that while he can do a lot, God doesn't expect him to be all things to all people. Dad needs to delegate more jobs even when he feels he may be able to handle them. Understand?''

"Yeah. And Mom—'' Jack said, ''we're with you all the way.''

C H A P T E R

3

Good News
and Bad News

With you all the way.

Jack's promise mocked, sang, and repeated itself in his mind until he felt the five words had been branded into his skull. They went to school with him in the few remaining days before Christmas vacation started. They went to church with him. They whispered him to sleep and shouted him awake—prodding, teasing, pleading for priority status in every moment of his life.

Much of the time he was so involved with helping Flis keep the house going while Mom spent long hours at the hospital that he could let them lie. Yet those words had a way of creeping into his mind just when he should be concentrating the hardest on homework and tests. Finally he shouted to an empty, snowy field, "I'm doing everything I can, for crying out loud! Mom says that if we keep our grades up and the house warm and meals made it's the best gift we can give her just now. If ever Dad gets to come home, then . . ." He stopped, appalled. What was he saying? If *ever* Dad gets to come home? Of *course* Dad would be coming home—maybe in just a few days. Their family prayer every night was for Dad to make it home in time for Christmas, and the doctor had cautiously said it might happen.

"Then how come Mom still has shadows in her eyes when she

comes back from visiting?'' Jack demanded of a snow-capped fencepost. He pulled his mouth into an ugly twist. If anyone saw him out here talking to fenceposts, they'd ship him off to the loony bin.

''So who cares?'' He kicked at a hard lump of snow. Somehow it helped. He didn't want to let Flis know how worried he was, although he'd just bet she knew anyway without him ever saying a word. ''How come it had to be Dad anyway, God?''

The next instant the thought came into his mind, *So who would you want it to be?* Feeling ashamed, he kicked another gob of snow into flying pieces and headed home. But that night instead of feeling miserable about Dad he made himself remember that thought. Would he really wish Dad's trouble on someone else? *No. Yes. Well, maybe, if it meant Dad would be OK again.* Jack didn't know if he felt better or worse. What kind of guy was he—frantically praying that nothing bad would ever happen to him or his family? What about all the other kids and their families? He really didn't want bad things to happen to them either.

Then one afternoon just before Christmas Mom came bouncing in wearing a Grand Canyon-size smile. ''Guess what! Dad's coming home—tomorrow.'' She looked like a kid with a giant lollipop. Every trace of tiredness had been erased by the good news.

''Great!'' Jack grabbed Mom and swung her in a wild race around the long living room. Felicity joined in, and out of breath and laughing, they finally sank into chairs.

''We'd better get as much done ahead of time as we can,'' Mom reminded. Little stars twinkled in her dark eyes. ''We haven't made fudge yet or strung popcorn or cranberries or . . .''

''Take it easy, Mom.'' Jack gently pushed her back into the chair when she started to hop up.

''We can do those things,'' Felicity giggled. ''Why bother with fudge? People keep bringing and bringing stuff. We've got enough candy in the freezer to last through next spring.''

''Yeah,'' Jack felt his own grin spread over his freckled face. ''We just thanked everyone and dumped the stuff in the freezer—I mean, after wrapping it up.'' Funny, he felt about 20 pounds lighter than he had an hour before. Worry sure got heavy after while.

GOOD NEWS AND BAD NEWS

That night the three knelt on the rug in front of the fireplace with its glowing coals. Mom prayed, thanking God for the wonderful news and for His loving care in whatever might lie ahead. For a second Jack's keen ears caught a faint tremble in her voice, and fear swooped back the way a hawk swoops after a baby chick. What wasn't she telling them?

Felicity must have missed the little quiver in Mom's voice. Her thankful prayers bubbled up and spilled over into the quiet room that was lighted only by the fire. They made Jack think of a rushing mountain stream in spring, eager to pour over the rocks and get to the sea. When his turn came, he managed to mumble, "Thanks, God." A hundred phrases teased then retreated. "Uh—for everything."

The moisture on Mom's and Felicity's lashes showed they felt the same specialness he did. Unwilling to break it, Jack waited until Flis headed for the shower before demanding, "OK, Mom, let's have it. You gave us the good news. I know there's something else."

"I do, too." Felicity had slipped into a robe, and anxiously knotting and unknotting the tie belt, she stood in the living room doorway.

"You're too observant," Mom said as she moved to the middle of the couch and held an arm out to each of them. When they sat down she looked first at Flis then at Jack. "I didn't want to spoil tonight because it is good news. Dad *does* get to come home for Christmas." She took in a long, unsteady breath. "But after that he's going away, for a long time."

Pure terror sprang into Felicity's eyes, and Jack thought his heart had permanently stopped.

"You mean he's going to *die?*" Felicity grabbed her mother for support. Her chalky face against her dark hair and eyes hurt Jack even through his own misery.

A stricken look crossed Mom's face before she exclaimed, "Oh, no, that's not it at all. My dears, I'm so sorry!" Color slowly crept back into Felicity's face, and Jack's heart pounded with relief.

"I just meant that Dad is weak, and this cold climate's the worst thing for him just now. He needs several months where it's warm and dry to heal that awful cough and get built up again."

"Thank God! I thought . . ." Felicity burst into tears.

"Me, too." Jack reached across Mom and patted the shining dark head. "Going away's no big deal. We'll have Christmas together then something will work out."

"I certainly hope so." Another worry wrinkled Mom's smooth forehead. "But we don't have to think about it yet. Let's just spend the Christmas holidays being happier that Dad's so much better."

Had there ever been a better beginning for Christmas? Jack couldn't remember one. The morning of Christmas Eve day found Dad stretched out on the long couch in the fir-scented living room. Fat red candles, waiting to be lighted, stood on the mantle. A happy fire danced and crackled and cast sparkling red and yellow and orange reflections. Felix, content at last, lay curled in the curve Dad's body made, his gravelly purr mixing with soft carols playing on the stereo. Dusty had been allowed inside, and Jack had brushed his red coat until it rivaled the flames *and* Jack's hair as they lay together on the floor in front of the fire.

Jack's mind kept as busy as he knew Mom and Felicity were in the kitchen. They'd turned down his offer to help and had sent him to keep Dad company. Jack grinned. Dad's even breathing under the colorful blanket they'd thrown over him to keep any draft off showed that he slept.

"I never knew before how much I took Dad for granted," Jack whispered in Dusty's ear, low enough so he wouldn't disturb his father, "or how empty the house could feel without him."

Dusty licked his friend's hand, and the boy whispered again, "Wonder what's gonna happen now, about Dad and going away and everything?" A squiggly feeling shot through him, but he determined to forget it at least until after Christmas.

Dad's morning nap proved valuable. As Jack told Felicity later that evening, "I bet half the congregation either stopped by or called today."

"I know." She looked serious, too old for 13. "He's tired, too."

"Yeah."

Jack glanced across the room at Mom, caught her look then nodded significantly at Dad. Her gaze followed his, then she laughed and gracefully said, "We really appreciate you folks dropping by, but we're going to have to let this man rest so we'll let you get home to your own family for Christmas Eve."

Boy, is she ever tactful, Jack thought and smothered a laugh. *I'da probably just said, "Hey, people, Dad just got out of the hospital, so give him a break and come back some other time, OK?" No wonder everyone says Mom's the perfect pastor's wife. She knows what to do and how to do it right.*

Christmas Eve ended with the Nelson family singing carols and thanking God for His goodness. Christmas morning started with a good breakfast of hotcakes and home-made maple syrup. "Enough to hold us until dinner," Mom laughingly told them. But Jack noticed she had dishes of raw vegetables and fruit tucked away in the fridge in case anyone got hungry in between.

Warm sweaters, bright scarves, heavy gloves, and many other thoughtful gifts covered chairs and the piano bench before Jack discovered a special gift back in the corner behind the tree. "New skis!" He touched their shining surfaces.

"You've grown so much, your old ones are too short and we found a real bargain on them," Dad told his son.

"Flis can have my others. They'll be perfect for her and go great with her new boots." Jack noticed how pretty Flis looked in the green sweater he'd bought her. She sat on the floor trying on the ski boots and laughing. Just for a second Jack wished it could always be this way, just the four of them together, having a great time. Then he shrugged. Life moved on and always would. Today would become a memory, and sometime he'd tell his kids and grandkids about it. Laughing at his own seriousness, he checked the wall mirror to see if he'd aged any, but the familiar face that looked back didn't show even one gray hair.

December 24 had been perfect. So had December 25. But on the 26th the sky fell in. Literally and otherwise.

The family awoke to steel skies that crouched above them then sent pouncing snowflakes to add to what already waited on the ground. At first Jack and Flis loved it. No need to head for the mountains when they had plenty of snow in far-more-than-usual amounts right at home.

Across fields, down hills, cold air and exercise kept them outside most of the day. Jack's new skis skimmed through the snow, giving him more speed than he'd ever achieved with the old ones. Felicity's cheeks matched her scarlet cap and scarf that showed so brightly above her white ski jacket. Jack's former skis gave her the correct balance, and the day's practice added immensely to her skill.

In the rush and swish of skiing, they ignored the weather until Flis finally admitted, "Even with all the clothes I have on, I'm freezing! Let's go home."

Jack realized how cold the day had become. Snow no longer fell, but a wind straight down the Columbia Gorge tore at scarves and hats, penetrating layers of clothing. "It's going to be *c o l d* tonight," he predicted and hurried after Felicity's flying figure. The lights in the windows at home looked super, and the smell of chili teased his nose until he could barely wait to shuck off his clothes, shower, and head for supper. Yet even while he stuffed himself until he groaned, Jack noticed how quiet Dad acted at the table.

"You feeling OK?" he asked.

"I'm all right." Dad's smile did the final job of warming Jack up. Nothing much could be wrong when Dad smiled like that.

"Then how come everyone's so quiet?" he persisted, still across the table.

"We need to talk after supper."

Now what? Jack didn't say it out loud, but the question perched on his shoulder all the time he helped clear the table and stack the dishwasher while Mom and Felicity put stuff away.

All traces of Dad's smile had vanished by the time the others joined him in the living room. "You know I have to get away from this cold as soon as possible," Dad started.

"Uh huh." Jack dangled a piece of yarn to tease Felix, who grabbed at it and stood up on his hind legs then rolled over with his treasure when Jack let go.

"Your mother and I have been concerned about just how we'll manage things. There's so much to take into consideration." Dad sighed and stared into the fire.

What did he see there? Jack wondered. *Weeks of doing nothing*

*when he was used to being active all the time? Days filled with sitting
around in the sun instead of visiting people and preparing sermons
and working?* He sure couldn't see how Dad would make it. Bor-ring.

Dad continued, "We want you to know that whatever we decide
to do will be decided because we feel it's the best for all of us. Or
maybe I should say it's making the best of things."

Jack abruptly stopped pestering the cat and sat up straight.
Something in Dad's voice had run up a warning flag of trouble. The
way Flis jerked to attention betrayed her awareness too.

"You've told us everything the doctor said, haven't you?" Jack
said as he leaned forward and fixed his gaze on Dad. "I mean, about
you're going to be all right and that stuff?"

"Absolutely."

Jack let out the deep breath he hadn't known he'd been holding.
"Good. That's all that's important, isn't it?"

"We're glad you feel that way," Mom put in, even though faint
shadows smudged around her eyes.

"Of course we feel that way." Flis set her chin in a firm line. "So
tell us the rest."

Dad relaxed. His thin hands lay still on his lap. "Here it is in a few
words. It's good news and it's bad news."

"Isn't it always?" Jack muttered and Felicity glared at him.

"The good news is that our own church youth leader, Tim, has
written to his parents who live in southern Arizona, not too far from
Phoenix. Mr. and Mrs. Chiles are practically insisting that we fly
down there as soon as possible, probably right after the holiday rush
is over and stay until summer." Dad made a face. "I can't see that it
will take that long to get me back in shape, but the doctor says it will."

"Tim's folks don't have any of their own family home now,"
Mom added, "and they're opening their hearts and home to us."
Something bright glittered in her eye and fell to her lap.

"That's pretty neat of them, huh." Visions of cactus and low
mountains and tumbleweeds raced through Jack's head. "Do they live
on a ranch?"

"No. They do have some land but they're retired and go traveling
during the hot summer months, then enjoy their *hacienda,* that's a low

Spanish-style house, in the winter.''

"I feel as if I'm running away from so much unfinished business,'' Dad complained. "We're just getting new programs going, and I have articles waiting to be written, and . . .''

"And all you need to land back in the hospital is to sit here—or in Arizona—and think about all that stuff,'' Jack told him.

"You're right. But it still doesn't make going any easier.''

Jack slanted a glance at Felicity's drooping figure. Going meant missing the last half of the school year in Vancouver, leaving ski opportunities and school activities, and trying to make friends for just a few months. It meant more to Flis than it did to him. Jack flopped back on the rug, hands crossed behind his head. It might be kind of exciting, taking off and spending time in a place they'd never visited. If they couldn't ski, they could do other stuff—swimming and maybe even horseback riding.

He turned on one side and faced Dad and Mom. "Do they have a swimming pool, or horses, or anything?'' He gave Flis a glance that warned her not to complain no matter what. Dad's health came first. Even if they both hated Arizona, it was up to him and Flis to do what Dad had said—make the best of it. Of course, it would be nice if the Chiles' place had fun stuff but if it didn't—well, May or June would come anyway. Feeling smug about his possible sacrifice, Jack quickly added, "Not that it matters. Flis and I'll be in school most of the time, anyway.''

Mom sat up straight, opened her mouth, started to say something, and closed it again.

Dad suddenly looked old and tired. His eyes filled with understanding and sadness when he looked at Felicity, then Jack. "Remember that I said there was good news *and* bad news?''

They both nodded.

Dad continued in the same quiet voice. His eyes showed how much it hurt him to say, "The bad news is that the Chiles have only a small guest suite big enough for your mother and me. Jack, Felicity, you won't be going.''

32

Splitting Up

The room rocked. Jack felt the same way he had once when he was little and had stepped off a merry-go-round. Not sick or dizzy—just disoriented. "Not going?"

"You mean we're staying here?" Felicity's eyes got round and she caught her bottom lip with her upper teeth.

"That's right. There's no room for you." The flat statement hung suspended in the room.

"Then we'll have to work something else out." Jack jumped up and stuffed his hands in his jeans' pockets. "I mean, we're a family and if you have to go somewhere, Dad, we go with you."

"That's right." Felicity joined the attack and belligerently stood next to her brother.

"I appreciate the way you feel, but there's nothing to work out. Your mother and I have exhausted every possibility. The only thing we can do is to accept the Chiles' invitation—and leave you behind."

"That stinks!" Jack's flaming temper slipped out of the control that he'd been trying to develop ever since Dad got sick.

Even usually sunny-natured Felicity cried out, "It's not fair! We've waited and prayed for you to get better and now you're going to desert us."

"That's enough." Mom's lips set in the straight line that meant, no more. "No one ever said life was always fair. We're doing the very best we can to help Dad get well. You two need to start thinking about that instead of how this is going to affect you. You don't hate staying behind any more than we hate leaving you, and when you complain, it makes it harder on Dad—on both of us."

Suddenly all the watching and waiting hours she'd spent at the hospital, the determined cheerfulness, the fears she must have had, rose to accuse Jack. Felicity expressed his feelings, "I—I guess we're being pretty selfish."

"Oh, honey, we understand, but there just isn't another choice."

"But what are we going to do?" Jack asked through stiff lips. "I mean, you'll be gone for months—and that's OK 'cause it means you'll get well, Dad."

"We haven't worked everything out yet." Dad leaned back and closed his eyes. "Remember, no matter what happens, God will be with *all* of us." He got up and said, "I think I'll get to bed. Don't worry, kids. Things will be all right."

Jack wanted to run after him and tell him how sorry he was for acting like a 4-year-old instead of a 14-year-old but Mom stopped him with a glance and a quiet, "Let him go, Jack. He feels terrible about this whole thing. He even wants me to stay here with you."

Jack saw the look on her face and knew she was being pulled two ways. He gave her a hug and said, "That's dumb. He needs you a whole lot more than we do. Flis and I'll have each other and . . ."

"Let's talk about it later." Mom drooped. "Dad and I have a lot more to settle before we'll be ready to come up with the best plan."

"Why did she cut you off?" Felicity wanted to know after Mom had followed Dad to their room.

Jack carefully put the fire screen in front of the fireplace, checked all the doors as he'd been doing every night for weeks and said, "I don't know." Felicity's anguished look followed him to bed an hour later when they turned out the lights and said good night. How would it be having not only Dad gone but Mom too?

Stop being a baby, Nelson, and go to sleep, Jack told himself. Surprisingly, he did, wishing that when he woke up, Dad's illness and the Arizona trip would be all a bad dream.

A day passed. A second. When Jack and Felicity asked if Dad and Mom had decided what to do with them, their parents just shook their heads. Late the second afternoon Jack signaled his sister to follow him to her room. When they got inside he closed the door tightly and said, "Look, we'd better get an idea fast or who knows what'll happen."

"What's that supposed to mean?" Felicity threw herself down on her puffy bed cover and looked at him.

"It means that Dad and Mom are thinking up some crazy scheme."

"How do you know that?" She acted like she didn't believe him.

"I overheard Mom say, 'Oh, dear, if they aren't together I don't know what they'll do,' then Dad answered but it was too low for me to hear." His heart thumped at the memory.

Flis didn't even accuse him of eavesdropping like she usually would have done. Instead she jumped off the bed in a hurry and slid to the rug next to him. "You mean we're going to get *separated?*"

Something in her voice and eyes made Jack feel a whole lot better. They might argue, and he might get jealous of her, but for a sister she wasn't so bad. "Maybe."

"That's terrible. It's bad enough for Dad to be sick and Mom and him to be taking off for Arizona without us but . . ." she turned and buried her face in the bottom of the bed cover.

"I've been thinking," Jack said slowly. "Why can't we go to an academy that accepts boarding students? At least we'd have each other if things got rough."

Flis turned a rainbow-after-rain face to him. "That's so cool! Why didn't we think of it before? Let's go tell the folks your idea. I'll just bet they'll be relieved." Some of the radiance left her face. "I wonder why they haven't said anything about it. They must have thought of a boarding academy."

The same squiggle of worry that went everywhere with Jack and prodded him now and then gave a sharp jab now. "I don't know." He took a deep breath, held it, and let it out. "I guess there's only one way to find out. C'mon." He held out a hand and helped her scramble to her feet. She deserved the unusual courtesy from him for letting him know how much she wanted them to stay together.

"Dad, Mom," Felicity took the lead when they reached the living room and dropped down next to the couch where Dad lay. Mom looked up from the mending in her lap.

"We've decided—I mean, Jack and I—" she looked at her brother for help.

"Could we go to a boarding academy while you're gone?" Jack blurted out.

His sweaty fingers curled into fists but relaxed when Dad said, "We've considered it."

An ocean-sized wave of relief washed through Jack. "Where will we go? Auburn, or . . ." his voice trailed off when he saw the expression on Mom's face.

"We weren't going to say anything until things were settled," Dad told them. "Felicity, we feel the best place for you *is* at Auburn Academy." He paused.

What about me? Jack screamed inside but he couldn't get the words out.

"Isn't Jack going, too?" Total shock crossed Felicity's beautiful face.

"No."

How could one word change hope to hopelessness? Jack wanted to protest, demand an explanation. But not a word would come out.

Again his sister spoke for him. "But why?"

Dad's eyes darkened. "Felicity, I think your mother and I should discuss this with Jack alone."

"Let her stay." *Had that growl come from him?* Jack wondered.

"All right." Dad shifted his body so he faced them better. "We love you a great deal, Son, but you do have problems getting along with people—especially people your own age. We can't be wondering how you're doing while we're thousands of miles away and not here to change things if they don't work out." Dad let him have it head on.

"And I suppose good ol' Flis is so perfect you don't have to worry about her being at boarding academy." All the past couple of years' bitterness overflowed. Even his joy at her wanting to be with him couldn't stop his hurt. "She's always been more of the family pet than either Felix or Dusty. Well, don't worry about it. Let her go. I don't care." He knew it was a lie when he said it, and the way Felicity bent her head and picked at her fingers didn't help at all.

"I don't want to go to dumb old Auburn, anyway. Sam at school will be glad to have me stay with him for the rest of the year, maybe forever—since you don't want me."

"That's not fair and you know it!" Felicity's head came up with a snap. Her angry dark eyes showed how hurt and upset she was. Good. If he had to feel rotten, she might as well, too.

"No one ever said life would be fair," Jack mimicked Mom's comment from a few nights before.

"We've heard quite enough from you, Jack." Dad's lips set in a straight line. "If your mother and I needed anything more to convince us of your immaturity, this little scene has certainly clinched it. There's no way we're going to inflict you—and your uncontrolled temper—on Auburn Academy *or* on any of your school friends."

"That's right." Mom backed Dad up all the way. For a fleeting second Jack remembered how he'd promised Mom to be with her all the way. Now a wall 10 feet high had grown between him and his family. He added a few more bricks by saying, "I'm old enough to take care of myself," and raced out of the room, down the hall, and to his own room, making sure the door slammed and the lock grated loudly enough so the others could all hear from the living room.

What should he do now? He dropped to his bed and let anger roll through him. Run away? Naw, that was dumb to even consider. A 14-year-old kid couldn't get away with that, especially a kid as short as he was. Besides, his red hair and freckles would make it easy for the police to spot him. What *could* he do?

For a long time Jack lay on his bed, wildly considering all kinds of impossible plans. Finally the quiet of his own room gave him an idea. Of course! That was it. He should have thought of it right off.

He unlocked his door, slowly went back to the living room, and faced the three who hadn't moved from their places but looked like figures who'd been placed in a game of Statues. "Sorry I acted like I did," he mumbled, planting his gaze on Felicity. "It's just that with

37

everything like it is, I got mad when you acted as if you liked Flis more than you did me.''

Mom's level glance didn't warm the way it normally did when he apologized. ''We always love you, Jack, but when you act in unacceptable ways we don't like what you're doing one bit.''

''I know.'' Suddenly he felt even more miserable. Was it his fault Dad looked so wornout? The last thing he needed was a bratty kid mouthing off. ''I don't always like me, either,'' he confessed.

''It isn't *you* but the things you do wrong that aren't likable,'' Dad reminded. ''Now if you can sit down and act human,'' he grinned, and Jack's sore heart started to heal, ''we still don't have it settled about the next six months.''

''I thought about it while I was in my room.'' Jack dug a toe into the carpet. ''Why can't I stay right here at home and keep on at school? There's plenty of food in the fridge and freezer, and I thought maybe Flis might want to stay, too. We're not babies and we could keep things going. Remember how good we did while you had to be with Dad at the hospital, Mom?''

Felicity came alive. Her face glowed and she bounced up and hugged Jack. ''That's perfect!''

''Sorry, kids,'' Mom's sad voice cut through their reunion. ''It just won't work.''

''Why not?'' Jack had prepared for a long siege to convince Dad and Mom it was the only way to go.

''First, you're too young to leave alone that long.''

''Don't you trust us?''

''It isn't a matter of trust. Teenagers need an adult around. Things come up that you simply aren't prepared to handle,'' Mom patiently explained.

''Couldn't we get someone to stay with us? Maybe an older person from church who'd like to be with kids?'' Flis asked hopefully.

Dad shook his head. ''Finding such a person on such short notice would be almost impossible. Besides,'' a troubled look clouded his expression, ''we've been fortunate enough to rent our house furnished until the middle of June.''

''You've got to be kidding!'' Jack forgot his role as a cooperative, mature person. "People are going to be in here pawing all over *our* stuff, living in *our* house?" The whole idea gave him the creeps.

"We'll be taking our personal things such as clothes, sports equipment, and the like. Everything else stays." Dad sighed. "Look, we're going to need the money. We can't expect the church to continue paying my full salary for six months when I'm not working. Even if they wanted to, I just wouldn't feel right taking it. Once I get rested some, I intend to try and write a few articles or maybe stories for some of our publications, but money's going to be tight."

Did Mom's sharp eyes see clear into his heart, Jack wondered. So many times it felt like they did. Now she said, "All it will cost us while we're gone is the transportation. The Chiles' have been just wonderful. They say they're tired of rattling around alone and she's anxious to have us there. I'll help her cook and clean, of course, but she and her husband are absolutely refusing to take anything for staying with them, even for food. We'll have to pay for Felicity to be at the academy, but," she turned pleading eyes on her son, "Jack, the only choice we have for you that we can afford is to send you to live with Grandpa and Grandma Nelson at Cottonwood."

"You mean go to the farm?" Jack bit his lip when he saw Mom's face. He knew it bothered her and Dad that Jack didn't get along with Grandpa. Visions of the old-timey farm that looked like something out of a TV western pranced in front of Jack's stunned eyes. Located in the coastal mountain range of Oregon not far from McMinnville, Cottonwood itself had always appeared half asleep the few times Jack visited his grandparents.

"Be a good sport," Felicity hissed in his ear. "Look at their faces."

Jack pulled himself together and even managed to produce a sickly grin. Then he croaked, "Hey, there's one good thing about it. I can take Dusty, can't I?"

The overwhelming relief in Dad and Mom's faces made his sacrifice easier. Jack grabbed Dusty, who had been drowsing in front of the fire, and rolled over and over with him. "Hear that, dog? You're gonna be a country dog, instead of a soft city mutt. Why, you might even learn to be good for something more than just petting. You can help me bring home the cows and all kinds of farm stuff.'' He continued talking in a monotone to Dusty until the other three held their sides from laughing.

"What about Felix? Does he go, too?" Felicity eyed the big cat who sat calmly washing his face and observing them through knowing slanted eyes.

"Sure. I bet he'll be a good mouser. Remember last summer?" They all laughed again.

Mom had shared the story when Dad had gotten home from a visit. Felix had cried at the back door, and when Mom went to let him in, he rolled and purred and looked totally pleased with himself. On closer inspection, Mom found that he'd caught a mole.

"Why, Felix, what a *good* cat you are," she had told him. She had patted him and had given him extra food, and all day he had trotted around after her.

A few days later, *scratch, scratch.* There stood Felix, going through the same routine. A dead mouse lay on the garage floor. Again Mom had praised him for being such a good cat and mighty hunter.

The third time Mom had heard the scratching at the door, she knew what to expect. She opened the door, and Felix leaped and rolled and performed the same antics as he had before. But this time when she looked down to see his prey there lay a long night crawler!

"I guess he thought he was doing something super," Flis had defended the cat, but she'd also joined in the laughter.

"I can just see Grandma's face when Felix the Great brings an offering of a night crawler to her," Jack said now.

His smile faded. How long it seemed since the night of the youth meeting when he'd determined to do something so he could be P.K. the Great and make Dad and Mom and Flis proud. *What if all I can do is come up with something no more important than Felix's night crawler?* he thought. *Felix felt he'd done something wonderful when it really hadn't amounted to anything. Of course he did catch a mole and a mouse, too. Wonder if I can—not catch a mouse or mole—but do something that is important? Maybe just helping Dad get sorted out and to Arizona is at least a "night crawler" in God's view.*

"Be a good sport," Flis had said.

At first Jack didn't know if he could. A dozen times in the next few days he wanted to yell and protest. Now that academy had ended for the holidays, it seemed the greatest place on earth. What would public school be like? Would the kids like him? He scowled. Who cared what a bunch of country hicks liked or didn't? He'd better be thinking of how to get along better with Grandpa—the tall, older edition of his own red hair and freckled face. Maybe if he weren't so short and Grandpa so tall, things would've been better. The way things were it always seemed like Grandpa towered over him, disapproving and ready to criticize.

Jack's good sportsmanship wore pretty thin when he let himself think of what lay ahead. Six months of Grandpa was one grim proposition.

Cottonwood Ranch
— Ready or Not

The few days remaining in the Nelsons' Vancouver home both raced and dragged for Jack.

Sometimes he wished he could just get it over with, tell everyone goodbye, and start what he privately called his "six months farm prison sentence." The sooner it started, the quicker it would be over.

At other times he wanted to grab time by the shoulders and hold it back. Each tick of the clock mocked him, "Soon, soon, soon," until he wanted to smash something. Most of the time he covered up pretty well. Why fight what couldn't be changed?

The one real bright spot came when Flis said, "Jack, if you want me to, I won't go to Auburn Academy. I'll ask the folks to let me go to Grandpa and Grandma's with you."

He started to make a smart remark about "family pet" or "people who get to make choices" but the drooping way she stood with one foot thrust forward stopped him. Instead he said, "I thought you were hot for Auburn."

"I was—when I thought we'd both be going." Her long, dark eyelashes lifted and showed how badly she felt about the whole thing.

"Oh." Jack struggled to overcome the fresh spurt of anger that they both couldn't go to Auburn.

"Do you want me or don't you?" Color stained her thin cheeks. She suddenly looked like a little girl again, the little girl who trustingly followed her big brother wherever he went, always happy just to be with him.

Jack cleared his throat. "Sure, I want you, dummy. Think Dad and Mom will go for it?"

"I think so." Tremendous relief showed in the way her tense figure relaxed. "I can help Grandma in the house and stuff while you work with Grandpa outside."

"I just can't wait to start mucking out the barn." Jack held his nose and made a face. "Anyway, let's go ask."

They needn't have worried. Dad and Mom not only thought it a great idea but Dad admitted, "This was our original plan so we could save money."

"How come you didn't say so, then?" Jack demanded, firing up like a car motor on a cold morning.

"If you remember, about the time we discussed all this, you were—shall we say—not feeling too friendly toward your sister."

Dad's crisp response brought hot color beneath Jack's freckles. "Oh, yeah. Guess I wasn't."

"We also knew how much Felicity wanted to stay in one of our church schools," Mom added. "Of course you did too but it just didn't seem practical."

Jack bit his lip but hid his irritation at the memory by announcing: "News flash. Listen up, Felix, Dusty. Felicity Nelson, star of Vancouver and the Columbia River, will be joining us in our—" he started to say *exile* but hastily substituted, "—in our trek to Cottonwood. Roll out the red carpet. Sound the alarm. I mean welcome. Ta-ta-ta ta ta ta!" He bowed low, one hand on his stomach the other spread wide. "Heeeeere's Felicity!"

"You're a nut," his sister told him, but the happiness in her voice told him how effective his acting had been. After that, things got a little better.

"One thing, they have horses. We'll get to learn to ride," Felicity

43

grinned. "I remember once Grandpa stuck me on the back of a horse when I was small, and I felt like I'd landed on the Empire State Building it was so far to the ground."

"What you need is a pony so small your legs can touch the ground on both sides," Jack kidded her.

She just laughed. "Yeah, then if I got wobbly I could keep putting one foot down the way I did when I was learning to ride a bike."

Still, by the time they'd packed what they wanted to take to the farm and on the night before Mom planned to drive them down to Cottonwood, Jack felt lower than the bottom snowflake in a six-foot drift. One good thing, the cold weather had been replaced with familiar western Washington rain so the driving wouldn't be hazardous.

"Got your skis ready?" Felicity called from her room. "Cottonwood's at higher elevation than here so we'll probably get in some good skiing."

"How can you sound so cheerful?" Jack lounged in her doorway and frowned at her.

"Why not? Things could be worse."

"I don't know how." He wasn't about to be comforted.

"Well, I could still be going to Auburn Academy, and . . ."

"Maybe you should be!" he growled, and was sorry the minute he'd said it.

Felicity's light mood vanished. "Look, I don't *have* to go to the farm. If you're going to gripe for the next six months, I won't go, either. I'll go to the academy, and you can live at Cottonwood by yourself if that's the way you want it!" She put her hands on her hips and stuck out her chin.

"Don't be dumb. It's bad enough having Dad and Mom gone. We have to stick together."

"Not if you won't try. I asked God to help us not hate it so much and I'm doing what I can." Her lips trembled.

"So why didn't He just make Dad better in the first place?" Jack's grudge against God still plagued him.

"Mom explained that," Flis went back to stuffing a few last-minute things into her pouch purse. Then she stopped and said softly,

44

"God's done a whole lot and you'd better believe it. How else could we wind up with having a nice church family *just happen* to get transferred into this area and *just happen* to need a place to live until they can look around for the right house to buy? Why don't you forget your bad mood and start thanking God that total strangers who might be anyone won't be living here and using our furniture? It's a good thing for the leasers, too. They'd stored their own furniture and planned to take a furnished apartment. This way they won't feel as pushed. They're paying a fair but not too-high price and the money will help us."

"Is this sermon number 41 or 106?" But Jack couldn't help grinning. God *had* worked out a whole lot of details in a real short time. "What was your original question, by the way?"

"Skis." Flis rolled her eyes at his poor memory.

"Yeah, they're ready. I'm sure glad the new people don't have little kids. It's easier knowing teenagers will be in our rooms than if they were sticky-fingered curtain-climbers who write on walls."

"Uh huh." Flis changed the subject. "Know what? I couldn't believe Dad and Mom insisting that we go to the youth meeting tonight. Seems like they'd want us to be home when we won't see them again after tomorrow for six months."

"That surprised me, too. Even when we said we'd rather stay home, they wouldn't hear of it." Jack considered for a minute. "You don't think the church kids are doing something for us, do you? I mean, it's not like we were moving away forever or anything."

"I thought of that too." His sister's eyes sparkled. "Could be. Since Dad and Mom decided to go ahead and get us down to Cottonwood before the new semester starts even though they don't fly out for another couple of days, there was plenty of time for word to get around." She carefully took her green Christmas sweater out of a dresser drawer. "I'm not counting on it, but just in case—I did save this out to wear tonight! I'll pack it tomorrow morning before we leave."

"Great minds run together. I left out my new ski sweater." Jack ducked when she hurled a small pillow at him. He even whistled while he got ready for the meeting.

"We'll have to act surprised if there is something," Flis whispered after Mom dropped them off at church and they stood just outside the door.

"I know." Jack grinned tormentingly and put one hand to his heart before saying in a falsetto, "Really, this is such a surprise!"

Flis giggled and shoved him inside.

"Surprise!"

The almost-full room had been decorated with balloons and *Bon Voyage* signs. Someone had sure gone to a lot of work. Jack noticed that tonight people paid as much attention to him as they did to his popular sister. The meeting itself went great. Tim had a lot of plans to discuss for the new year. Every time some neat idea came up, Jack died a little inside just knowing he wouldn't be there for it. But in the fun following the discussion he joined in and made himself part of things more than he'd done for a long time. He didn't try to boss but just blended in as one of the crowd.

The evening ended with special devotions. Tim turned off all the lights except a couple of candles. He invited anyone who wanted to say something to speak up. Several of the kids mentioned how much they'd miss the Nelsons but how glad they were that Pastor Nelson would be OK.

Jack struggled to his feet. "Uh, I don't want to go. I have to, though. And—knowing you're all here waiting for us to come back helps." He stopped for a few seconds before adding, "Dad and Mom say God's always with us, so we're gonna be OK. Thanks for tonight." He waved at the decorations, the devastated plates of cookies, and fresh vegetables and dip. "It means a lot."

Felicity said just a few words, then Tim called for a friendship circle. Hands joined, they sang, "God Be With You Till We Meet Again." At least, most of them sang. Jack couldn't get one word out of his tight throat, and he'd just bet Felicity couldn't, either.

When they got home, Flis hung her wet coat in the bathroom to dry, and Jack spread his out on a chair by the baseboard heater. "You knew, didn't you?" Flis accused her parents.

"Of course." Dad's pixie-grin lightened his thin face.

"Thanks for making us go." Jack sat down on the stone hearth. The fire felt good on his back.

"Any time." A look of understanding flashed between father and son. Jack knew that in all the long months ahead he'd remember and be strengthened by it. Dad *did* know how hard life was for a 14-year-old, short, red-setter-looking P.K. Somehow it made a whole lot of difference.

The look gave Jack courage to hug Dad the next morning and say, "We're gonna make it. All of us," and feel the same love and warmth and understanding of the night before. "I know," Dad said, and again Jack knew he did.

As if to make up for the coming separation, sunshine streamed over the soggy world. Dad needed rest instead of a long drive, so the other three climbed into the Toyota. Jack held the front door for Mom and gruffly told Flis, "Get in front. I'll keep Dusty company. Think Felix will be all right?"

"Sure." Flis caught the big cat up in her arms, scratched behind his ears, then buried her face in his fur. If she watered him with a few well-hidden tears, he didn't seem to mind. Once inside the car, he settled into her lap, purred, and fell asleep before they'd crossed into Oregon.

Dusty wanted to stand up and look out, but Jack coaxed him down. Mom didn't need a dog blocking her rear view. She drove as competently as she did everything else, and Jack could hardly believe it when they got to McMinnville. "It always seemed like it took forever when I was a kid," he said. "I guess everything's more of a big deal then, huh?"

"Oh, I don't know." Flis pressed her nose to the window and Jack followed her gaze toward the high school with its empty, vacation look. Too bad they wouldn't be going to school there. It looked big enough to get lost in the crowd if the kids didn't like him. But not the Cottonwood High School. Sprawly, also Christmas-vacation-empty, it didn't look like it could hold more than a hundred or so kids. Jack's insides twisted. It would be his first experience with public school. Flis's, too. *Just remember,* a little voice whispered, *six months isn't forever. You can handle it.* But for some strange reason Jack felt relieved when the school disappeared behind them, and they headed out of town toward Grandpa and Grandma's ranch.

"There it is!" Flis shouted. Felix leaped to her shoulder and peered out the window. Dusty chose that time to start barking up a storm. He climbed all over Jack and peered out at his new home.

"Knock it off!" Jack told the dog, and forced him to lie back down, although Dusty showed signs of mutiny. The minute the car door opened, Dusty almost knocked his master down as he headed for freedom.

"I forgot it was so big," Flis whispered while Jack untangled himself from the closely packed back seat.

"Yeah, I always want to call it a little ranch instead of a farm." Jack stepped out of the car and took a new inventory. What with Dad's busy schedule, it had been easier for the older Nelsons to visit in Vancouver than for Jack's family to get out to Cottonwood, so it had been a long time since they'd been there. Now he breathed deeply. One thing, the air was sure neat—pine-scented from the trees on the rolling slopes not far from the house. No flowers yet, and patches of snow still clung to the ground under the biggest trees. A few horses grazed in an enclosed pasture. Red and white Hereford cattle along with some Holstein cows dotted the fields and slopes.

Jack shifted his gaze from the blue-looking distant mountains toward the log house on a slight knoll behind him. Although it had two stories, it hugged the ground and blended into the gently swaying trees behind it. Grandpa said it could have been a stage stop if it had been a few years older. He'd fallen in love with the place when he was a young man. He'd saved his money, worked hard, and bought it when land prices were lower. Gradually, he'd added enough livestock until he didn't have to work on other jobs but could get a modest living from the place itself.

I wish I could be like him. Wow, what a weird idea, Jack thought. *I'm too much like him already! That's why we don't get along very well. Maybe now that I'm 14, we will. We have to. We're stuck with each other for six months.*

His involuntary shudder got him off to a bad start. Instead of running to greet his grandparents the way Flis did, Jack held back. By the time he got up the neatly graveled walk that wound between flower beds, now brown and uninteresting, he only said, "Hi, Grandma. Hello, Sir."

Grandma smiled through her glasses. Her simple dress and large white apron showed where her work interests lay. "Welcome, Jack. We're so glad you're going to be with us."

Her tall, rusty-haired, freckled husband gave his grandson one of those measuring glances Jack hated before he said, "Think you'll be any good around here?"

Jack missed the twinkle in the eyes so like his own and heard only the challenge. His square chin set, he muttered, "I may just surprise you."

"Good." For a moment a heavy, workworn hand rested on the boy's shoulder, then a gruff voice ordered, "Take your stuff upstairs. Felicity, last room on the right. Jack, across the hall from her."

Smarting from what he considered a poor welcome, Jack lugged suitcases and skis and tennis rackets upstairs. Every time he saw Grandpa watching his progress, he frowned, but made sure Grandpa didn't see him. He could just bet what the older man was thinking: that there wasn't time on a farm for kids to spend in all that foolishness—skiing and stuff. By the time he'd hung up his clothes in the big closet, stacked his other gear in corners of the old-fashioned but spotless and cozy room, Jack's mouth turned down and his mood matched it. He clumped downstairs after checking to see if Flis and Mom were still there. They weren't, but the pretty room lay in perfect order. It already looked like Flis, with its dainty spread, small rocker by the window and a desk with a good light.

"Pretty, but I like mine better." He had to admit the room that would be his new home for the next half a year had a lot going for it. It was twice as big as the one back home, and he could see over hills, past a shining stream, clear to the mountains beyond. Felicity's room faced the opposite direction, and its sparkling windows framed the tidy front yard, the curving road toward town, and at least a dozen cottonwoods waiting to get new spring leaves.

"At least we've got privacy," Jack mumbled to himself. "Our rooms are great. If I ever have time off, I can explore those hills. I

49

mean, after I learn to ride.'' He refused to recognize the insistent little voice that whispered in his heart, *So if it's all so great, how come right now you're so homesick that it feels like someone hit you in the chest with a basketball?*

C H A P T E R
6

Just This Side
of Sneaky

"Shhhh," Jack whispered in Dusty's ear and took another cautious step up. Dusty followed. One stair after another they crept, silently, slowly, until they reached the upstairs hall. Good. Just a little farther, and—

"Dusty, shut up!" Jack ordered his whining dog, but the damage had been done.

Grandpa and Grandma's bedroom door swung open. Grandpa's tall body cast a gigantic shadow over the sneaking pair. "What did I tell you about dogs in the house?"

"He's not hurting anything. Besides, it's his first night here, and he shouldn't have to be outside in the doghouse." Jack turned sullen. Stupid rules.

"You're the one who's in the doghouse, Jack. We explained to you that we just don't have animals in the house. We never have. We never will. We expect you to respect our feelings while you're staying in our home." He held out one big hand. "Now, are you going to take Dusty out or shall I?"

"I will." Jack shut his lips hard and tugged at Dusty's leash. "Come on, you."

Dusty whined again, and Jack complained all the way downstairs and out to the brand new, warm doghouse on the big covered back porch. "Troublemaker. It's all your fault. Why couldn't you just keep your mouth shut? And why does Grandpa hate dogs? At least, he doesn't like them enough to let them inside."

Dusty didn't help a bit. He just crawled into his new home and peered out at Jack as if to say everything was cool. Felix appeared from somewhere and stalked into the doghouse after Dusty. He curled between the red setter's paws and purred.

Instead of making Jack feel better, it made him madder. "Traitors. Go ahead and like it. I don't have to." He marched back inside.

"Don't, forget to lock the back door again," Grandpa called. Jack viciously shot the dead bolt into place and climbed the stairs, not making any effort to be quiet this time.

"Goodnight, Jack," Grandpa said.

"G'night." But his grandson didn't look at him. Instead, he skulked to the cozy room he now hated and stared out into the winter sky. Six months of this. Yecccch. Even after he shivered and crawled under the warm blankets, his anger and hurt and even some shame for trying to deceive Grandpa kept him awake.

A thin stream of light fell over his bed. He sat up. Now what? Had Grandpa decided to come bawl him out some more? Well, he'd had it for one night. He shoved his head under his pillow and hoped the night visitor would get lost.

"Jack?" Felicity's fingers raised the pillow.

"Whaddaya want?" He flipped over. Moonlight showed his sister all bundled up in a robe and slippers.

"It's kinda lonesome."

She must miss Felix, Jack thought. All he said was, "Yeah."

"I heard what happened. My door wasn't quite closed." She plopped down on the foot of his bed and hugged her arms around herself.

"Grandpa's so stubborn. Why did he have to get a grudge on against Dusty—and Felix—anyway?"

"He didn't. You know that. His own dogs and cats sleep in the barn, yet he built that super doghouse for our pets."

"So?" Jack wasn't about to be coaxed out of his anger.

"So if every time you and Grandpa disagree there's a big fight, how are we ever going to live here until June?"

Jack didn't have an answer. As usual, Flis got him with her logic. Her face shone pale in the dim room. "Jack, if I say something will you get mad?"

"Depends on what it is," he told her grumpily.

"I won't say it unless you promise."

"Oh, all right. It's probably the only thing that'll get you outta here, and I'm tired." He propped up against his pillows and pulled the covers clear up under his chin.

Flis sat quiet so long he wondered if she'd changed her mind. "Are you going to say something or aren't you?"

She took a long breath, held it, then let it out. "I just thought—I mean, Dad and Mom wouldn't let you go to Auburn or stay with a friend because of your temper."

Jack started to argue but she reminded, "You promised," and he stopped.

"Look, Jack, back in Vancouver the kids all knew you. They put up with your bad moods and your trying to boss everyone 'cause it was a Christian school and people are supposed to act the way Jesus would. You have to admit you come on like Superman."

For a second Jack felt like pushing her onto the floor. Yet something in Flis's voice told him she was only saying these things to help. It didn't make him feel any better, but at least he listened. "So?"

"So we're going to a brand new world out here in the hills. These kids aren't going to be bossed by some city kids who transferred into their school for a semester. If we want to fit in and be part of things, we're going to have to earn our way, not just be accepted because Dad's the pastor."

"Where do you get the *we?* You really mean *me,* don't you?" he accused, but kept his voice low. They sure didn't need Grandpa or Grandma to come barging in.

"Doesn't what I just said make sense?" Flis ignored his bitter question. She leaned a little forward. Her eyes looked like deep hollows in the partially lighted room. *"Neither of us,"* she emphasized the words, "can expect everyone here, including Grandpa and Grandma, to change. We're the outsiders. It's up to us to fit in with them, not the other way around."

"Think I'm going to be a wimp and follow people around like a puppy dog? No way!"

Felicity just stared, then said, "Do what you want. If I have to live here for six months, and I do, then I'm going to try and have some fun. I can't see spending six miserable months. If you have any sense, you'll start taking a good, long look at yourself. Maybe you won't like what you see." Her concern turned to anger. "You're so disgusted with Grandpa being stubborn, it's almost funny. You're just like him, Jack Nelson, only you won't admit it!" She slid off his bed and stood next to him like some upset angel. "Go ahead and pout the rest of this winter and spring. Who cares? I'm going back to bed. When I get up tomorrow I'm going to help Grandma all I can. The next day when we start school I'm going to be as friendly as I can, too. Not just 'cause I want to fit in, but for a whole lot more important reason."

"And just what's that, preacher?"

"Because Jesus expects us to. Get this through your dumb head. We may be the only kids from a church school that Cottonwood High ever gets. If we act rotten, they're going to judge Jesus by us." She whirled. Her slippers whispered over the floor. The crack of light from the hall got wider, then disappeared. But Jack lay awake a long time thinking about what she'd said.

Breakfast came two hours before he was ready to crawl out of bed. Flis looked sort of cute in a big apron Grandma had wrapped around her—over her jeans and sweater. Jack had to admit the hot biscuits, honey, and home-canned peaches were the best.

"Glad to see you stuffing yourself." This time Jack did see the twinkle in Grandpa's eyes. "We have a busy day, and it's a long time until dinner."

"Don't you have lunch?" Jack's eyes opened wide.

"We call it dinner and the evening meal's supper. By the time you've worked all morning you'll want more than a small lunch," Grandma told him.

Was she ever right! First, the cows had to be milked. Range cattle made up most of the herd, so the few cows that provided milk for the family's use didn't require a milking machine. Jack's private expression when he watched Grandpa milk, then first put his hands out to learn was, "Gross!" But he held his tongue, gripped hard, and after getting red-faced and embarrassed at his lack of skill, finally got the knack. Thin streams of milk sang into the shiny bucket, and although Jack thought longingly of the rows and rows of boxed and bottled milk in the supermarket, he kept on until he could get no more.

"Go to the next cow, and I'll strip this one," Grandpa said.

"Strip?"

"Finish up." The older man's more powerful hands squeezed again and again, bringing down milk long after Jack thought the cow must have been empty.

If Jack thought milking was gross, he couldn't even find a word awful enough to describe mucking out the stables. He discovered it was impossible to hold his nose with one hand and still use the pitchfork. He tried holding his breath as long as he could against the pungent, barny smell. When he finally breathed, a great rush of odor threatened to choke him.

"Whew! Am I glad that's done." He surveyed the clean straw he'd forked down after using the hose to wash away the last of the manure—and the smell.

In spite of the many things Jack hated about the farm, there were also things he liked, such as the horses that had come into the corral to be fed. He could hardly wait to learn to ride. As long as he was away from the cows, they weren't all that bad. The batch of kittens, half-hidden in the loft, tumbled and played. Would Felix discover them? The loft itself offered endless possibilities to hide if things got unbearable.

Well, he'd made it through one morning. Only how many to go? "Don't be dumb," he growled at himself and headed for the house. Grandpa had told him to get cleaned up for dinner, and he couldn't wait. No wonder they had to have more than lunch on the farm. It smelled a lot like Mom's kitchen and he hurried.

"I helped make the hot rolls," Flis bragged, a streak of flour on her cheek backing it up.

"They're good." Jack reached for another and held out his bowl for more homemade split-pea soup. Last night he'd gone from white anger to feeling hurt and deciding he wouldn't speak to his sister if she thought he was so terrible, to feeling he'd better treat her well. She could still go to Auburn Academy if he made her miserable here.

"Thanks. Grandma says I'm already a good cook. Now she's going to teach me to be a great one."

Jack saw the way Grandma smiled at his pretty sister, and a little pang of envy crept inside him. Just then Grandma smiled at Jack exactly the same way and asked, "Well, how's our new farm hand?"

He sat up in surprise. "Uh . . ."

"He's going to be just fine," Grandpa put in, and Jack had a warm feeling as the praise curled around his heart the way Felix curled around his shoulders sometimes. "Thanks, Grandpa. What do we do after lunch, er, dinner?"

Grandpa slowly buttered another roll, eyes fixed on it in concentration. "I think—"

Jack held his breath.

"I think if Grandma can spare Felicity, we'll have a riding lesson. It's cold but clear, and snow's predicted for later in the week so we'll make the most of today."

"I thought you were going to . . ."

Jack caught the quick shake of Grandpa's head toward Grandma before Grandpa said, "Yes, today's a good day to learn to ride."

"Super!" Jack forgot his grudges, and let his grin creep into a wide smile. "Can we ride to that little mountain?" He pointed out the window.

"Hardly." Grandpa laughed and Jack felt stupid. "It's a lot farther away than you think. Always remember that in this country distances can be deceiving. You may think a hill is just a little way off when it can be miles."

Flis laid her fork on her plate. Her enormous eyes held a little fear. "Grandpa, what happens if our horses run away and we get lost?"

"That probably won't happen, but if it should, always remember this: My horses are well-trained. If you'll let them do the deciding, they'll bring you safely home. Don't try and make them go your way.

56

Loosen the reins and trust in their God-given instincts to take care of you.''

Jack made a face to himself. *How could a dumb ol' horse find the way if a smart person couldn't?* But he didn't say anything or protest. After all, Grandpa was being pretty nice to show them how to ride.

"Is this all we get to do?" he demanded a little later. "Just put on saddles and take them off and put them on again?"

Grandpa's temper flared. "Look, young man, the most important thing you'll ever learn about horses is how to care for them and your equipment. Many a rider has had a bad spill because he didn't get the saddle on tight enough—or some other equally silly thing.''

"Sorry," Jack mumbled.

"Now, let's see you both do it once more."

Jack wouldn't admit how tired his arms were from throwing the heavy saddle over Old Prince, the enormous bay he'd been assigned. Flis had it a lot easier. The pinto Princess stood a lot lower than Old Prince. Grandpa's buckskin King matched the bay in size, and the pinto colt Jester wasn't old enough to be ridden yet.

"Looks good," Grandpa said after his pupils had finished. "Now, put your left foot in the left stirrup, give a little spring, and throw your right leg over your horse."

Flis managed it on the second try. Jack wondered if his short legs would ever make it, but to his surprise he slid into the saddle of the patient horse without more than a flick of Old Prince's ears.

Step by step Grandpa taught them about holding the reins, pressing the horses' sides with their thighs, and relaxing when they finally trotted around the inside of the big corral. "If you stiffen up, you jounce. Let your body melt into the saddle."

"Sure," Jack muttered, going up and down like a jack-in-the-box. But when Grandpa opened the gate and Old Prince swung into a faster but smoother motion that Grandpa said was a canter, Jack loved it. Cold air teased his face and chased away all thoughts of Vancouver, school tomorrow, even of how mistreated he was. Who could feel awful on a rocking-chair gaited horse?

His excitement lasted clear until bedtime, even when Grandpa announced that on schooldays all he'd have to do would be muck out and help with night milking. Still, the ghost of Cottonwood High School kept him from being content. He knew Flis would be in the same buildings. The school was so small that junior and senior high all shared the same classrooms, although they had their own classes. How would they receive a too-short, too-redheaded preacher's kid?

"Well," he told Dusty later when he went out to be sure the red setter and Felix had settled in for the night. "I can't get any taller by tomorrow. I can't change my hair. So—hey, why didn't I think of it before?" Determination filled him. There was one thing he could do, and he would!

The next instant his hopes shattered. *Flis would never go along with it in a million years, would she?* Jack stayed on the porch until he felt cold then went inside, still wondering how to get around Flis.

When all the lights had been put out except the one in the hall that served as a guide to the bathroom, Jack slipped into his sister's room. "Flis?"

He had to call her three times before she woke up and rubbed her eyes. "What's wrong?"

"Nothing, if you'll help me."

She reached for the bed lamp, but Jack grabbed her hand. "Don't turn on the light. It shows beneath the door."

"OK, but what are you talking about?"

"I've been thinking about what you said last night." What a great way to get her attention!

"And?" Moonlight showed her all huddled in her covers. Jack knew from her skeptical expression he had a big job ahead of him.

"And I want to be part of Cottonwood and fit in the same way you do. Tonight I figured it out. I can't dye my hair. Grandpa and Grandma would go bananas. I can't take magic growing pills and get taller."

Sympathy showed in Felicity's eyes.

It encouraged him even more. "That's two strikes. But I *can* start school here without the third strike already against me." He stuck his chin out. "The kids don't have to know Dad's a preacher."

"But he is!" Flis sat bolt upright in bed.

"So? You know how in class when new kids come, teachers

58

always want to have them introduce themselves and tell a little about what they like and who their folks are, stuff like that. When they ask me what my folks do, I'm going to tell them they're people-helpers.''

She looked at him like he'd gone crazy.

"It isn't a lie. They *are* people-helpers. Not like those TV guys who go out and do charitable stuff but . . . .''

Flis found her voice. "That's just this side of sneaky!'' she protested. "Besides, our records from the academy will show. It's better to be honest in the first place.''

"Give me a break, Flis! Girl P.K.s don't have it rough, but when you're a guy—remember some of the stories about the way they get treated?'' Jack watched her carefully. "All I have to do is avoid the whole thing—change the subject if some-one asks. The only thing is . . .''

"I knew there had to be a catch.'' Flis crossed her arms and glared.

"If you don't go along with it, it won't work.''

"You think I'm going to Cottonwood High School and deny Dad? You're crazier than I thought you were.'' Little red flags flew in her smooth face.

"Please, Flis. You don't have to lie. Just don't make a big deal out of it.'' He hesitated. "Will you at least not bring it up unless someone asks you and you *have* to tell?'' He wondered if she'd even answer him. First she turned her back on him, slid down farther into bed, then lay silent for a long time. When she spoke it sounded muffled.

"I don't think it's right. It isn't fair to the folks. But—''

Jack's heart leaped.

"I won't make an issue of it unless I have to.''

"You're great,'' he told her. "Someday I'll do something for you.'' He got away before she could change her mind. Just maybe tomorrow wouldn't be so awful, after all.

C H A P T E R

7

Blown Cover

The first school day of the new year sparkled blue and white under a cloudless sky that had dumped six inches of snow during the night, then had turned cloudless, repented, and smiled. Jack shivered in the frosty air when he went out to feed Dusty.

"Maybe there won't be any school," Flis said at breakfast.

Grandma just laughed. "There'll be school. We get a lot of snow and are prepared. The buses will all have chains on their tires and be ready to roll. Oh, it's kind of nice where we are. You can see the bus go up past us to several houses. It swings around in a lopsided circle, down a big hill, and comes back to our side road. You can get on there."

"How long is it gone?" Flis wanted to know.

"Between 12 and 15 minutes."

Jack wished it would get stuck on the hill and not come back until school was over for the day. Then he grinned at his own grouchiness. Putting off facing Cottonwood High School just meant staying tied up in knots that much longer.

Getting on the bus turned out to be a letdown. The juniors and seniors sat in the back and didn't pay any attention to the two new students, except to glance over them before going back to discussing a thrilling basketball game the team had won during Christmas vacation. Only about two-thirds of the seats were filled, so Jack sat down halfway back, and Flis took a separate seat a little closer to the front.

"You're the Nelsons, aren't you?"

Jack turned. A sleepy-eyed boy behind him opened his eyes a little more and grinned at Jack's surprise. "Everyone knows you're going to be here until June, and why."

Great! Was his cover blown before he'd ever established it?

"Really?"

"Sure. Small towns are nosey—I mean friendly." Mischief danced in his blue eyes. "Besides, we're the Nelsons' closest neighbors. It's only about a quarter mile."

Jack bit his tongue to keep from showing his amazement at calling someone who lived a quarter mile away a "close" neighbor. He already liked this kid and didn't want to act dumb. "What's your name?" he asked.

"Dick Smalley." The sleepy blue eyes looked Jack over. "Although you're the one who oughta be named Smalley, huh?"

Jack felt his face turn to match his hair but managed a weak smile. "Yeah. Dad says I'll start growing any time now."

"I grew four inches last year," Dick bragged, then added, "it sure feels good not to be such a shrimp now. Know what I mean?"

"Wish I did!" Jack couldn't help scowling.

"Aw, don't worry about it. Cottonwood doesn't care, especially since we're just freshmen. Hey, your sister's cute, isn't she? Cuter than my sister—that's her, talking to your sister."

"I think they're both cute." Jack checked out the blonde girl chattering away with Flis. "She looks a lot like you."

"Thanks a lot," Dick said sarcastically, but Jack knew it pleased him even though he wouldn't admit it.

By the time the bus unloaded at school, Dick had already promised that he and his sister Karen would take Jack and Flis sledding after school.

"I don't know if we can go," Jack said.

"Don't you want to?" Dick's eyes opened wide. "We have great hills and stuff. Do you ski?"

"Sure, but I have to help with the milking and muck out and stuff."

"Big deal. I do, too, but there's always at least an hour or more between when we get home and chore time."

"Good. We'll ask Grandpa, but I'm sure it'll be OK."

Dick grinned tormentingly. "Naturally. I'm such a neat guy and such a good influence the Nelsons will be glad to have me look after you."

This time Jack's smile glowed. If everyone at Cottonwood High turned out as neat as Dick, school would be a piece of cake.

"Uh, just what does everyone know about our being here?"

"Your dad got sick and had to go to where it was warmer, so the Nelsons got stuck with you." Dick cocked his head to one side and smirked,

"Good." Relief flowed through Jack.

Right away Dick pounced on it. "How come good? Do you have some terrible secret no one knows about?"

"Of course not." Jack nearly dropped his new notebook he laughed so hard.

"Hey, Karen, wait up." Dick obviously forgot what they'd been talking about. "This is Jack Nelson."

"It's going to be so neat having you at the farm," Karen said, her blue eyes smiling the same way her brother's did.

Suddenly Jack could add truthfully, "I think it's going to be fun, too." He noticed how Felicity struggled to hide her shock and how she quickly said, "I guess we're all going sledding after school, huh?"

"Yeah." Dick took charge and herded them toward the front door, down the hall, and to the principal's office. "You'll have to get registered and stuff. See you later." He whistled as he headed toward his locker.

It didn't take long in the office, and before the tardy bell rang, Jack saw Flis disappear into her first class and he loped toward his. Now came the test.

"Jack Nelson will be with us this semester," the attractive teacher said. "Anything you want to add, Jack?"

He slowly stood, hating the blush he knew made him look like a stop sign. "Just that . . . ." his mind went blank. Someone giggled and he tried again. "Uh, it sure is pretty here, and it looks like good skiing and sledding and stuff."

He sat down in a wave of laughter, but Dick called, "All right," from the other side of the room, and Jack found himself laughing with them. Funny how much better it felt than when they'd been laughing at him.

For a whole week he avoided any mention of Dad's job, though a few times he almost slipped. It sure was hard not to say anything to the Smalleys. They spent almost every afternoon together and often evenings, when they studied, popped corn, or just talked. Dick and Karen acted like the Nelsons' coming to the farm had to be the greatest thing since peanut butter, and their parents treated Jack and Flis the same. Once Mrs. Smalley said, "We were a little worried when we heard kids from Vancouver were moving in. We should have known anyone related to Grandpa and Grandma Nelson were all right."

"What does she mean by that?" Jack whispered to Karen, who had been sitting next to him and teasing Felix.

Karen rolled her eyes. "You wouldn't believe the trouble we had last summer. A family rented the place on the other side of us. The kids were into drugs and their parents drank. We get it even here in Cottonwood but not like this! The police busted them and they left. The whole town was glad." Twin dimples showed when she added, "See why we're suspicious of you big-city folks?"

Jack almost blurted out the truth but bit his tongue just in time. Yet he felt guilty. He hadn't lied or anything, but he sure knew the Smalleys would think it strange if they ever discovered what he'd planned.

Cottonwood High really was a neat school. The principal demanded high standards. The townspeople backed him. Any student caught messing around with drugs knew he was automatically out. Anyone caught smoking got suspended for three days. If a kid got into drinking, it meant no sports, debate team, or anything else. It didn't stop all problems. Yet it did go a long way toward having a unified student body and terrific school spirit.

Just when Jack started to breathe easier, it happened. The Smalleys and Nelsons decided to put their suppers together and everyone stuffed themselves. Mr. Smalley caught Jack unprepared when he said, ''Why didn't your dad stay on the farm? Seems like once a person lived out here, he wouldn't want to ever live anywhere else.''

''He—he likes to help people.'' Jack fumbled for words, hoping Grandpa's excellent ears weren't tuned his way. ''He works a lot in Portland, distributing food and clothes and finding shelter for poor people.''

''That's a wonderful thing to do. Is he a social service worker?''

''Kind of. Well, not exactly. I mean—''

''Who's for more pie?'' Grandma called from the other end of the table. Jack felt he'd been given a reprieve. He also felt just the way Peter must have felt when he denied Christ. *I didn't lie,* he reminded himself. *Dad does do all those things. I'm surprised the Smalleys didn't know Dad's a preacher. I guess they moved in a long time after Dad left, and Karen said until we came the families were friends but didn't really visit that much.* Still he felt guilty.

He felt even worse when Dick came up a few days later at school and demanded, ''How come you lied about your dad?''

Jack stalled for time. ''What do you mean?''

''I mean Felicity told Karen the truth.'' Before Jack had time to get angry with his sister, Dick added, ''I'd be proud of my dad no matter what he did. Are you ashamed or something?'' Scorn underlined every word.

''Of course not.'' Jack ducked his head then forced himself to look straight into Dick's flashing blue eyes. ''It's just that being a P.K. isn't easy, and when you're short and red-haired and freckled, it's worse.'' Words spilled out from behind the dam of Jack's resentment.

''Your sister doesn't feel that way.''

''She doesn't have to. She's dark and good-looking just like Dad and Mom." Disgusted at himself, he turned his back on Dick then whirled to face him again. "What made Flis tell? She promised she wouldn't."

Dick looked a little more understanding. "Karen helps the school secretary sometimes, filing and stuff like that. She saw your transfer records."

"And I suppose she spread it all over school!"

"Don't be totally stupid," Dick flared. "She just asked Felicity. I'll tell you one thing, though. You'd better start telling the truth. Otherwise, when the kids here find out, they'll figure that if you act like there's something to be ashamed of, there really is. Wise up, Nelson." The bell rang and he walked away, leaving Jack to stare after him.

Snow followed clearing. Clearing followed snow. The four friends skied and sledded the same as before, but Jack knew things couldn't be the same—unless he admitted he'd been wrong. The only thing he wanted more than Dick and Karen's respect was not to be put down at school. So far no one had paid much attention to him either way. Karen involved Flis in the junior drill team and choir, but Jack hovered on the edge of things, torn between wanting to participate and being afraid of not doing a good job. Finally he decided to do something about it.

His chance came when his class discussed the freshman fair booth. Each class had the responsibility of coming up with a booth for the annual school fair that raised money for extra-curricular trips, sports equipment, et cetera.

"Last year's freshmen did fish pond," someone commented. "Shall we go with it again?"

"Why don't we do something *really* neat?" Jack asked. "Something different from whatever's been done before."

"Like what?" The class president eyed Jack.

He wished he'd kept still. "Uh—like maybe appointing a committee to make recommendations. It's kinda hard coming up with ideas in just our short meeting today."

"Good idea. You can be the chairman, since you suggested it. You've got a week until our next meeting. We have to decide then.

Any other new business? If not, the meeting's adjourned.''

Jack chose Dick, another boy, and two girls for his committee members. ''That way I won't vote unless it's to break a tie,'' he told them. ''Can we get together tonight?''

''Sure, at our place,'' one of the girls offered. Jack's head nearly burst with ideas all through the rest of the school day and during supper and chores. Mr. Smalley dropped him and Dick off about 7 and said he'd be back at 9.

Jack called the meeting to order and started pouring out all his ideas—everything from trying to get a former Cottonwood resident who became an author to come back and sign books to having a bake sale.

''Get off it,'' Dick said good-naturedly. ''People here can't afford that author's books at $14.95 plus tax. And the 8th graders have already spoken for the bake sale.''

''Oh.'' Jack thought fast. ''Well, any other ideas?'' The usual fish pond, dunk tank, and similar activities were suggested. ''Look,'' he told them. ''We want to do something really different. In Vancouver, we—''

Dick gave him a warning glance. ''Vancouver's a lot bigger than Cottonwood.''

''So I noticed,'' Jack said sarcastically, unwilling to give up what he considered his great ideas. ''Why even the acad—the private school—I attended was—''

''You went to private school?'' The other boy lifted his eyebrows. ''Figures. What is it? For weirdos? Or for snobs too good for public school?'' All thoughts of the upcoming fair fled. The academy suddenly became the super place he'd never felt it to be when he attended. ''No. It's a church school, and it makes Cottonwood look like something left over from dinner. My dad says . . .''

''Who cares what your dad says? Who's he? Some do-gooder who goes around poking his nose in people's business? We know what social workers are like. One of them came out here last winter and wanted to know why Cottonwood didn't 'take care of its own' instead of having loggers draw from the unemployment money *they'd paid ahead of time!*'' Ray glared at Jack.

"Dad isn't like that!" Jack jumped up and put his hands on his hips. "He's not even a social worker. He's a minister."

"Big deal." The boy also stood up. He towered over Jack. "No wonder you're like you are, runt. A preacher's kid, went to a dumb old church school—this meeting is adjourned, forever." He grabbed his coat and headed outside with Jack right behind him. They reached the front yard. Jack twisted free from Dick's hold and ignored his, "Forget it." Instead, he took a flying leap, tackled the tall boy, and they both rolled in the snow. "Take it back," he yelled.

"No way." His opponent got Jack flat on his back, sneered, and said, "My dad says people who send their kids to private schools aren't any better than communists."

"Shut up!" Jack tried to free himself and couldn't.

"You're the one who started it." A hard fist landed on Jack's nose. He felt blood spurt. Sickness crawled through him, and he barely heard Dick holler, "That's enough. He started it. You finished it." The heavy weight rolled off him and Jack lay in the snow, dazed, unbelieving. What would Grandpa say about this?

"You OK?" Dick helped him up.

"Yeah." Jack touched his nose. It didn't feel broken, just bigger than Pinocchio's. *He'd got his by not telling the truth,* Jack remembered. Ouch, it hurt.

"Better have the doctor look at you," one of the girls called after them when they refused to come in but waited outside for Mr. Smalley. "I'm sorry things turned out like this."

"So am I." Jack had never felt so thoroughly ashamed in his life. Some witness he'd been. If Cottonwood judged church school kids by the way he acted tonight . . . He held the wad of paper towels Dick had grabbed tighter against his nose and said a thankful prayer when Mr. Smalley showed up early.

"Not broken, but badly bent." The doctor announced after a thorough examination. "Just be glad the other guy didn't pack a heavier wallop."

Jack didn't think it was funny. Neither did Dick, for he said on the way home, "Better decide how you're going to act tomorrow."

"What's that supposed to mean?" Jack couldn't get his mind off his aching nose.

"If you go to school acting like everyone was to blame except you, it'll be the worst thing you can do," Dick warned.

"So what am I s'posed to do, get down on my hands and knees and beg? Is that what you'd do?"

"Naw. I'd just admit I was in the wrong and not be afraid to stand up and say so. That way, the kids will respect you."

All night Jack suffered. He'd managed to sneak upstairs without anyone seeing him, but tomorrow would bring a reckoning: with Grandpa and Grandma, the kids, especially Felicity. "I suppose everyone will throw up to her what I did," he groaned. By morning he'd slept some and thought a lot more—and reached a decision. He woke Flis before daylight, waited for her to settle down from seeing his ugly nose, and told her the whole thing. He freely confessed to Grandpa and Grandma, starting with hiding the fact he was a P.K. and going from there.

"So I acted stupid. You don't have to tell me. What are you going to do?" he ended by saying.

Grandpa looked at Grandma. His eyes twinkled and reminded Jack how much they were alike. "I'd say you've already suffered enough, wouldn't you? God often has a way of letting us experience the consequences of our own actions. The important thing is, what next?"

"This." Jack marched to the phone, grabbed up the directory, hunted a number, and dialed. "Uh, Ray? This is Jack Nelson. I just want to say that last night was my fault. I deserved what I got." He listened in silence. "Forget it. Our committee still has to decide on the fair booth." Another silence, then, "OK. See you at school. Tell the girls we'll eat lunch together and talk."

He slowly hung up the phone, hardly daring to look at the others. When he did, tears and smiles mingled on Felicity's face. A tender look showed in Grandma's eyes.

And Grandpa? Curiosity changed to approval and something deeper when he asked, "Just wondering—have you measured yourself lately?"

Now what did he mean by that? Jack scratched his curly head. "No, but part of me has grown, that's for sure." He patted his still-swollen nose and laughed, surprised to discover that neither hurt as much as he expected.

8

Rapiding

Hey, Nelson, where'd you get the nose?" someone called from the back of the bus the next morning.

Jack gritted his teeth, started to yell back, then caught Dick Smalley's anxious look. "From not keeping it out of other people's business," he said and laughed. For a second stunned silence filled the bus. Then everyone laughed, even the good-natured driver. For the second time Jack discovered that when he laughed first, and others laughed *with* him, it was far different than when they laughed *at* him. A week later his nose and other people's curiosity had gone back to normal. The second committee meeting went off great. Ray acted like Jack had become his best friend and made a big deal out of reporting to the class Jack's idea of having an on-the-spot, pizza-while-you-wait booth at the fair.

Early in February the snow disappeared, and the Nelsons and Smalleys switched their time together from skiing to riding.

"I'm really going to miss Old Prince when we go home," Jack told Karen one sunny afternoon and patted the big bay.

"Just Old Prince?" Sunlight glinted off her blonde hair and shone on her laughing lake-blue eyes.

"I might miss Dick, too." But he knew his face showed that Dick wasn't the only Smalley he'd miss.

"Why don't you stay on through the summer?"

"I guess we could." He let his gaze sweep over the rolling hills, distant mountains, and brave crocuses that had poked up through the hard ground even before the snow had melted and now bloomed lavender, white, and yellow. "If you'd said that even a month ago I'da laughed."

"People change," Karen's sidewise glance showed she meant it personally.

"Yeah." Jack could talk with her almost as well as with Flis. "Things are sure different at school. Guess the best thing that ever happened to me was getting socked."

Karen cocked her head to one side. "Sometimes God has to sock us, or let us get socked, to make us learn." She lightly touched her heels to her horse and sprang ahead, challenging, "Race you to the barn," and ending the heavy conversation.

Almost before it seemed possible, March flew past and most of April. One gorgeous late April day Dick came bouncing up. "Hey, wanta go rapiding with the guys?"

"What's *rapiding?*" Jack slammed his locker shut, glad for a no-homework night. The teachers must be getting soft, spring fever, maybe.

"It's cool." Dick's eyes lit up. "We start above town and ride the Cottonwood River rapids down to the deep pool below our place. You swim, don't you?"

"Uh—yeah." Jack hated to admit how scared he was of the water and he *could* swim—some.

"Piece of cake. C'mon, you'll love it. Ray and some of the older guys are going. This is your chance to show everyone your stuff," Dick coaxed.

"OK. You don't think Grandpa will care, do you?"

"Naw. We do it all the time. The rapids aren't that swift and the river isn't deep except at that one place. You climb out on the rocks there." Dick raced off to his next class, and Jack slowly headed in the other direction, wondering what he'd gotten himself into.

"Where's the inner tubes and air mattresses?" Jack whispered to

Dick when about a dozen guys hiked to the river after school the next afternoon.

"What inner tubes and air mattresses? We slide down on our bottoms and guide with our hands."

"You've gotta be kidding." Jack inspected the foamy river with its twists and turns and white water merrily cascading down past town.

"Watch Ray."

Jack did. Ray stripped down to his swim trunks, waded waist high into the river, sat down, yelled, "Wow, cold!" and away he went, laughing and sailing down the rapids like a human boat.

"It looks like fun," Jack admitted. "I'm not sure—" Splash! Splash! Body after body hurled into the cold water until Dick and Jack were the only ones left on shore. "Let's go. Want me to go first or follow you?" Dick asked, one foot already in.

"Wait until the other guys get around the bend so if I look dumb they won't see."

"Everyone looks dumb when they're rapiding. Let's go!" With a mighty yell Dick followed the others.

"I have to do it," Jack told himself, eyeing the river as if it were an enemy soldier. "They'll all think I'm chicken if I don't." He shivered his way into the water, clenching his teeth against the cold, then got in the half-sitting position he'd seen the others take. The next second he muttered through chattering teeth, "Of all the dumb ideas, this is the worst." But before he could even think about getting out, the rapid water grabbed at him and sent him flying. Down, down, he sped, using his hands as oars to push away from rocks on each side.

Never had he been so keenly aware of sensations. The cold air, the rushing water, the blurred vision of trees and bushes whipping by left him breathless. Once he caught on to what to do and stopped getting banged against rocks worn smooth by countless gallons of water hurrying on their way to the ocean, he even started to enjoy it.

Not for long. Unused to the hard farm work that had toughened the Cottonwood kids, Jack's strength couldn't equal the constant tug of the river. Even the muscles he'd been developing from pitching hay and straw down from the loft for the animals didn't keep him from fatigue. How far was it, anyway? A million miles? It felt like it.

RAPIDING

He rounded a wide curve and sailed into a straight stretch. "Thanks, God," he whispered through shaking lips. The other boys danced up and down on the rocks along the shore just above the deep pool Dick had mentioned.

Not far now. He could make it. Jack moved his arms, trying to steer toward the rocks. The speed of the river increased.

He paddled harder with his hands—and still hurtled down the rapids, straight into the deep, deep pool.

"Swim for it!" he heard someone yell.

Jack tried—and failed. He'd used up every ounce of energy. He sank.

Choking, spluttering, up through the icy pool he bobbed, flailing his arms and trying to kick.

He sank again.

An eternity of floating to the top, sinking, knowing he couldn't fight any longer ended with a terrific yank on his hair. If Jack hadn't been so half-frozen, he'd have yelled, it hurt so bad. Something flipped him onto his back. What felt like an iron band crossed his chest and towed him through the water then pitched him onto the sand and out of the river.

Jack retched river water. Had he swallowed most of the Cottonwood? A rhythmic in-and-out, in-and-out of his body finally brought him back to reality. The biggest senior sat astride him, pushing, releasing and pushing, releasing.

"I'm OK," Jack gasped, twisting under the strong hands. "What happened?"

"Crazy kid. Why didn't you tell us you could barely swim?" Ray didn't sound mad, just upset.

"I—I didn't want to be a chicken."

"You were almost a dead duck!" Dick shouted. His angry face and blue eyes showed that Jack hadn't been the only one scared. "Boy, I've seen a lot of dumb guys, but you've got to be the absolute dumbest!" He choked and some of the anger disappeared. "At first we thought you were showing off, bobbing up and down to prove what a great swimmer you were, or maybe even to scare us. Then Tim saw the expression on your face. Good thing for you he's a great diver. He grabbed you on what was probably your last trip down and hauled you out.''

"Th—thanks," Jack stuttered, and staggered to his feet. "Anyone got a blanket or anything?"

"Sure." The dripping senior wrapped one around Jack. "I brought clothes down earlier. Get in the car and I'll take you home." He sent a significant look at the others. "Pile in, everyone. It's a lot colder standing here now that we're out of the water."

Still half-dazed, Jack let Dick lead him to Tim's car. Even the powerful heater in the old restored Buick didn't warm up in the short drive to the farm. Tim and Ray and Dick had to half-carry Jack inside.

"What on earth . . . ." Grandpa came running from the barn.

"Jack!" Felicity pushed through the little circle of guys and grabbed his hand. *"What happened?"*

"I went rapiding."

"It's all over," Tim told the family. "He got too tired and had a little trouble getting out of the deep pool. We helped him. Just get him warm and he'll be OK."

A wave of gratitude toward the older boy threatened to swamp Jack. No one had uttered a word about how stupid he'd acted.

Before anyone could say more, Grandpa ordered, "Flis, go run the tub with as hot water as your hand can take." He picked Jack up and headed for the stairs. "Thanks, boys." Five minutes later he'd undressed Jack the way he would a baby and slid him into the steaming tub. Too tired to even thank him, Jack stayed in the water until his skin wrinkled and the lump of ice that his heart had turned into earlier started to melt.

"I—I can get out OK," he told Grandpa when a knock came at the bathroom door.

"Good. Supper will be ready. Can you come down or do you want a tray?"

Why had he ever thought Grandpa's voice sounded cold and crusty? Its tenderness finished what the river had almost done. Jack took a deep breath and held it then said, "I'll be down." He dried, crawled into the P.J.s and warm robe Grandpa had left next to the tub, watched the water swirl down, then slowly walked downstairs on rubbery legs.

Even before supper, Grandma gave him a huge mug of hot water, honey, and lemon juice. It slid down, warming as it went. Hot vegetable soup with homemade dumplings, applesauce, salad, and gingerbread followed until Jack protested, "When I swallow it goes uphill. I guess I'm through."

He lay on the living room couch near the blazing fireplace, vaguely hearing Flis and Grandma talking in the kitchen. Sounds of dishes and silver clinking suddenly grew precious. If it hadn't been for Tim—and God—one Jack Nelson would be lying on the bottom of a deep pool or dead on the shore.

By the time the kitchen work ended, Jack had made up his mind. He waited until Grandma settled in her favorite rocker and Flis perched on the end of the couch, close to his feet. "I want you to know what really happened." It came out in a sort of croak but he plowed on.

"Uh—it was great of Tim not to worry you, but he just told some of it." Jack glanced at Grandpa. Now was the time for the "I thought so" he'd seen shining in Grandpa's eyes.

"What's the rest of it?" Flis clutched her hands. "I'm not sure I want to know, but I guess we'd better."

In slow words with little silences tucked in between, Jack told how Dick had invited him to go rapiding. "It isn't his fault," he quickly added. "He asked if I could swim and I said I could. I can, some, just not enough. If he or the others had known what a weak swimmer I am, they'd never have let me do it." He stared at the flames and relived those awful moments. "It was freezing cold but not too bad at first. I even liked some of it. Then I got so tired, and it went on forever. Things got blurry. I came around the last bend and when I saw the guys already out, they looked like a bunch of angels! Just a few minutes and I'd be with them. I remember saying, 'Thanks, God' and knowing He got me through.

"It didn't work out. The rapids rushed faster. I tried and tried but I couldn't get to shore. Instead I got dumped into the deep pool. The guys yelled at me to swim. I tried to." He could see the horror in his sister's face. "It didn't do any good. I bobbed up and down, too tired to fight much."

"Did you give up?"

Jack shook his head. "No. I knew if I did I'd had it."

"Oh, Jack." Flis put her head in her arms and her shoulders shook. He knew this hurt her as much as what he'd gone through.

"I kept doing what I could, then Tim dove in and got me." He clamped his lips shut. No use making Flis feel worse by describing that sick scene on shore.

Grandpa poked up the fire and sent a shower of sparks up the chimney. "When you thanked God, you didn't know it would be for your life, did you?"

"No." Jack quickly looked at his grandfather then away.

"I'm not going to say anything more about your choosing to attempt something you knew you couldn't do, Jack. I do want you—and Felicity—to think about something. Do you remember the exact moment when you knew you wouldn't make it?"

Jack's throat dried to a crisp. "Yeah."

"Do you also remember the feeling of the strength behind Tim when he rescued you?"

"I'll never forget that." Jack could still feel that yank of his hair and the grip across his chest.

"When we come to the point in life when we know we can't make it on our own, God's strength reaches down and saves us through His Son, Jesus," Grandpa said soberly.

Grandma, who had sat quietly during the whole conversation white-faced and twisting a little handkerchief in her fingers, added, "If you'd refused to accept Tim's help, where would you be?"

"I don't want to think about it."

"That's what a lot of people now, especially kids and younger people, say." Grandpa's face looked sad in the firelight.

"I know that," Jack replied. "But I accepted Jesus a long time ago—when I was just a kid. So did Felicity."

"It's one thing to invite Jesus into your heart. It's another thing to let Him take complete control of your life," Grandpa told them. Shadows hid the expression in his eyes. "There are many ways of growing. Let's hope today showed you something you'll remember. God's love and mercy saw to it that Tim, who's an excellent swimmer, stood in the exact spot necessary to notice your predicament. Think about it.''

Jack did. All night he slept, rode the rapids, bobbed and sank, awakened, then repeated the performance. By morning he'd developed a groggy croak and a slight temperature. No school for him.

The day got worse. From the time he heard Flis leave on the bus, long hours stretched. His head hurt. His body felt sore and bruised. He didn't feel like reading or watching TV. Instead, he lay in his cozy room, glad to be alive and hating the thought of being honest with himself.

One thing he hadn't told his family and that was Dick yelling, ''We thought you were showing off . . . maybe trying to scare us.''

Just like the boy in the old fable who cried, "Wolf, Wolf!" to see the people come running. Then when a wolf really came, no one ran to save the boy, Jack told himself bitterly. *Show-off. Yeah. Dad and Mom knew it and wouldn't let me go to Auburn Academy or stay with friends. Flis knows it. Now Grandpa and Grandma and everyone here in Cottonwood knows about Jack Nelson, the not-so-great P.K.*

Grandma trotted up with juice and a good dinner, and Jack felt worse. She had plenty to do without having a big lunk like him to wait on.

All afternoon Jack faced his problems. How should he act when he went back to school? At least, there was a weekend in between. Maybe Dick and Karen had already written him off as hopeless. Were the kids putting Flis down because of him?

He could barely stand it until the bus came and Flis dropped her books and stepped into his room. ''What's everyone saying?'' he demanded.

The strangest expression settled on his sister's face. ''Is that all you care about, what the kids are saying?'' He stared at her scornful face, too shocked to reply.

''What they're saying isn't much. Even Karen doesn't know what really happened. Dick let me know the guys decided to keep their mouths shut. Not just for your sake, but because if it gets out, parents will ban rapiding for everyone, even those who are big enough to do it.'' Her usually smiling mouth twisted. "*Or* men enough to admit they can't swim well."

"I don't need you to hassle me," Jack spit out.

"Isn't it about time someone did?" Flis walked toward the open door, then turned back and looked at her brother. For a moment Jack thought, *She acts like a stranger. I never thought Flis would let me down, even if everyone else did.* Depressed, he closed his eyes and turned over.

The next instant her voice froze him. "Go ahead and shut your eyes. Turn your back on life and everything, even me. That's what you've always done. I don't know why I thought maybe things would get different!"

A Day Off

Jack and Flis had disagreed, argued, scrapped, and buried their differences a hundred times. Yet the same strangeness Jack had seen in her face warned him this time it wasn't the same. He flopped back over in bed. "What did you say?"

Flis set her lips in a thin, straight line. "You wouldn't want to hear it."

"Chicken!"

He regretted it the minute he said it, especially when his sister's face turned bright red and her eyes glared.

"That's it!" She banged the door, stalked to his bed, and let him have it. "I said you're a real coward. Not about stuff like being scared of the dark. But about living and being a human being and trying to show others the way Jesus wants them to live. Do you think you're the only person who ever hated things? Well, you aren't. We have it pretty soft. We've got great folks and a good home and friends. But you! You grouch around just because you aren't the tallest kid in the world. You complain because you're red-haired. If you'd keep still about it, no one would care. A lot of people have a lot more fears than you do—"

"You, I suppose!" Jack finally got a word in.

"Go ahead and be sarcastic. Yes, I do, if you want the truth. You're so busy feeling sorry for yourself you don't even notice."

"So what's the big problem on the little mind?"

All the fight drained from Flis. She drooped into a pitiful heap on the foot of the bed. "I'm afraid."

"Of what?" Jack raised up on one elbow, wishing he hadn't been so hateful even when she said those things about him.

"That Dad won't get well. Ever."

"That's dumb." Then why did his throat tighten?

"Is it? We get these cheerful little letters from Mom, but you notice she doesn't really say all that much. Just that Dad's slowly gaining strength." Flis reached in her pocket for a tissue and mopped her face.

"What's she supposed to say? That there's been a miracle and they're coming home a month early?"

Flis just shook her head. Jack didn't know what to do. He finally asked, "Why didn't you say something?"

"How could I?" Some of her spirit returned. "All winter I kept waiting for you to grow up. When Ray smacked you and you admitted you were to blame I really thought you'd changed. I needed someone to talk to so bad. Grandpa and Grandma are swell, but I've always looked up to you. Maybe I just wanted to lean on someone and have him tell me everything's going to be OK."

She cried harder. "Oh, Jack, why couldn't you be there for me? It's so hard, having everyone think I'm strong when I'm not. Sometimes, even God seems far away." Her voice trailed off.

If the roof had caved in on him, Jack wouldn't have been hit harder. He'd never suspected the pain Flis suffered. All this time while he had been eaten up with his own selfish feelings, his sister had been struggling with far more serious doubts.

"I'm sorry." It sounded small, worthless in the quiet room.

"I didn't mean to say anything. Then when you acted like almost getting drowned didn't mean anything, just what people would think, I couldn't help it." Flis blew her nose and looked at him through tear-drenched eyes.

"You probably won't believe it, but I'm glad you did," Jack said slowly, in his frog-like voice. "I never had any idea—and that's my fault for not noticing."

"The only thing that's really helped was knowing Grandpa and Grandma felt things had to get better. I've learned so much, just being here."

"Me, too." Jack knew he spoke truthfully. "If we'd stayed in Vancouver, maybe I wouldn't have had to face the things we were scared of." He blindly looked out at the peaceful mountains. "It's just that I want to be someone! Being a P.K. means everyone thinks you have to be an angel, or at least an example. I want to do something great or important."

"I know. So do I. I told Grandma that one day."

"Really? What did she say?"

Flis sniffled, "First she smiled. Then she said if I really want to be someone special, I have to choose the people I run around with. I asked her if she meant kids like Karen and Dick.

"Grandma shook her head. 'Start hanging out more with God,' she said. She was so serious I couldn't even laugh at the way she used our kind of language. She also said, 'One person with God is a majority. Everyone else without God can't ever permanently put down that winning combination.' "

"She's pretty sharp." Jack lay for a long time thinking about it. "So's Grandpa. That must be what he meant last night—you know, the difference between inviting God into our hearts and letting Him be in control." He squirmed. "S'pose if we start letting God handle things we'll feel better?"

"I feel better already." Flis slid off the foot of the bed. "Friends?" Her anxious eyes told Jack how important their little talk really was.

"Friends." He watched her cross the room, step into the hall, leaving the door open. He felt closer to his sister than he had since they were a whole lot younger.

Surprisingly enough, no one said much to Jack at either church or school about his adventure. A few kids asked how he felt after his ducking, and that ended it. The upcoming fair had taken priority over other things, and Cottonwood prepared for it by working as a community. Jack's "Piece of Pizza" booth idea caught on, and a lot of spare time went into constructing a booth, rounding up donations of ingredients, making a chart of who would work when, then tacking colored streamers of red, orange, green, and white to the open-fronted structure.

During the whole time, Jack worked hard—on the project and on keeping from bossing it. He let Ray and Dick and the others take charge, cheerfully following their instructions.

It paid off, too. The fair crowds zeroed in on "Piece of Pizza," and errand-boy Jack kept busy running for more supplies. The Cottonwood High School principal announced that the fair had netted more than it ever had before, and a lot of credit went to the school itself and to all the students who helped.

More letters arrived from Arizona. The good news that Dad couldn't wait to get home brought peace to them all, especially to Flis. Jack felt he had grown since December. "Too bad I didn't mark the wall," he told Flis. "I don't have anything to measure against."

She grinned. "Oh, I think you have a mark to measure yourself against—Grandpa!"

"Fat chance. It would take me a century to grow *that* tall. At least, I've, I mean we've, learned to ride. Still can't say I like mucking out, but it doesn't take as long as it did."

April bloomed its way into May. Still-crisp mornings did a quick switch into sunny, warm afternoons. Jack stayed subdued. Now the farm required a lot more work. Flis helped Grandma plant gardens. Jack sometimes felt the day should be 30 hours long to get everything done. At times he almost fell asleep over the Bible reading he'd started doing nightly after Flis had jumped all over him about his attitude.

In the months working with Grandpa, Jack had learned to respect him more than almost anyone else he knew. Not more than Dad or Mom, of course, but when he saw his tall "boss" surveying the horizon for weather changes, smiling at a new spring calf, or bowing his head at evening prayers, Jack couldn't help remembering how Flis called Grandpa someone to measure against.

As for Grandma, Jack never tired of her home-baked cookies, her stories of what he called "the olden days," and the way she smiled through her glasses.

Everything settled into routine, and Jack rejoiced over the progress he had made in controlling his temper. Then the peace of the farm shattered.

If only Dick hadn't wanted Jack to go riding with him! The teachers had an in-service day, which meant no school on a particularly inviting May Friday.

"Hey, wanta ride up the canyon with me?" Dick wanted to know on the telephone the night before. "First thing tomorrow morning."

"Do I ever! Just a sec." Jack covered the mouthpiece and asked, "OK if I go riding with Dick in the morning?"

Grandpa put down the newspaper and looked at his grandson with troubled eyes. "What about the barn?"

Thud. Jack's excitement hit the ground. "I could do it some other time." He knew what a weak statement that was. Every night the past week when he did a once-over-lightly mucking out, he had told Grandpa, "We've got Friday off and that morning I'm really going to clean this place up."

Grandpa didn't say a word, just kept watching Jack and waiting.

"Uh, I guess I can't go." Anger at Grandpa and at himself for putting things off and disappointment over not getting to go mingled, and when Dick coaxed, saying, "Sure you can. How often do you get to play cowboy?" Jack felt even worse.

"What do you mean, cowboy?"

"Well, maybe cowherder's better." Dick laughed. "Dad has a few cattle that always wander down and winter in the canyon. We bring them up in the spring." He paused. "How come you can't go, anyway?"

"I have to tackle the barn." He lowered his voice. "I've been just getting by all week and I promised Grandpa that tomorrow morning I'd make up for it."

"Just what you always wanted to do with your day off, huh!" Dick laughed again.

Jack asked hopefully, "Couldn't you go in the afternoon?"

"No, Mom made an afternoon dental appointment for me in

McMinnville. I have to leave about six and get back by two. It's a long ride, especially when you have some ornery critters wanting to graze along the way.''

Jack told his friend goodbye and hung up. Instead of letting it end there, he wandered outside and complained to Flis, who sat on the top front porch step playing with Felix. A string of barn kittens tumbled all over the big cat, but he didn't act like he cared. ''At least he and Dusty like it here,'' Jack muttered.

''You do, too, when you're not feeling sorry for yourself.''

''Knock it off, will you? It's bad enough having to miss the ride with Dick without you putting me down.''

''I'm not putting you down. You're the one who made the deal with Grandpa about cleaning the barn.'' Her maddening grin and teasing eyes sent new flames of anger licking at him.

''I s'pose you never break a promise.''

''No, I don't.'' She stopped teasing and stared at him.

''Why? Are you going to?''

For one exciting minute Jack considered it. Then he let his shoulders slump against the porch post. ''Naw.''

''Good.'' Flis checked him out then said, ''Want me to help you in the morning? You could get done quicker and ride partway down the canyon trail—it's not all that steep—and meet Dick on his way back.''

''Would you really?''

''Sure. I don't get behind in my work for Grandma, so I have plenty of time to do good things for others.'' She smirked and Jack acted like he was going to hit her but couldn't help admitting to himself that Flis really did what she said. Better organized, maybe.

Jack got up early the next day. By the time Flis called him to breakfast he'd already started his hated job. Forkful after forkful of straw came down from the big pile to cover the thoroughly cleaned floor of the stalls. He noticed one thing. It sure was a lot harder than usual. All week he'd avoided spending the time to really do it right. Now the corners that had been ignored offered time-consuming areas. No more. He gritted his teeth and dug in, making sure every trace of dirt got erased.

A DAY OFF

After breakfast Flis helped finish the job, and a little before 10 o'clock Jack headed for the saddle on the barn wall. "Old, Prince, here I come!"

"Looks good, Jack." Grandpa's keen eyes swept the now-spotless stalls.

"Thanks." Jack started to throw a blanket over the bay.

"Why—you missed something."

"What?" Jack shot a quick look around.

"The loft. Remember, the old hay has to be moved to one side so new can be put in."

"But we won't have new hay for months!" Jack protested, clutching the blanket. "I'll have plenty of time to do that." Why did Grandpa always just have to look at him and make him feel guilty about things? Why didn't he just say, "Look, you set the time to do it. Now get with it."

"Do I *have* to do it now?"

Grandpa's steady gaze never left his grandson's face. "That's up to you." He didn't wait for an answer, just went back out the wide-open barn door, leaving Jack and Flis staring at each other.

"I'll never get to meet Dick now." Jack viciously threw the saddle blanket in a corner and stabbed it with a nearby pitchfork.

Flis didn't answer. Instead, she crawled up the ladder to the loft, settled a scarf over her hair, and asked, "Where does the hay have to go?"

"The end away from the big window with the shutter over it. That's where the new hay gets put in." Jack sullenly followed his sister up the ladder and started moving what had to be half a million tons of hay. Flis tried to talk with him, but he didn't respond. Tantalizing pictures of himself and Dick rounding up cattle danced in the dusty loft along with motes of sunlight.

Hours of hard work later, Jack climbed down from the ladder. He and Flis had only stopped long enough to eat dinner.

"It's a shower for me," Flis sighed.

"Not me. I'm going for a ride."

"Now?" She glanced anxiously at the western sky. The sun had moved into the lower half of the sky. "Can you get anywhere and back before dark? Besides, it's almost supper time.''

Jack's fingers busied themselves with saddling Old Prince. "I'm not hungry. I can ride down to the river and get a quick swim in that shallow pool. I want to do *something* fun on my day off.'' He remembered how Flis had worked just as hard as he did. "Thanks for helping. Not that it did any good.'' He expertly tightened a cinch. "I still didn't get to go meet Dick.''

"So there'll be other times.'' She came close while he swung to the saddle. "I wish you'd wait. Even with daylight savings time, sunset isn't that far off.''

"I'll be back.'' He touched Old Prince with his heels, settled low in the saddle to enjoy his quick ride, and waved to Flis who slowly closed the big barn door and walked toward the house. Tiredness showed in her every step.

"She's a good kid,'' Jack told his horse. "Hey, how about a little speed, slowpoke?''

Old Prince easily changed pace to the long lope Jack loved. It didn't take long to get to the river. Jack carefully tied the reins to a tall pine, laid his jeans and shirt, boots and socks on the ground, and waded into the neck-deep pool. Cold, but nothing like the day he'd gone rapiding. He swam lazily for the few minutes it took to make him feel not so grimy, then he stretched out in the sun, soaking up its warmth. Boy, could he ever sleep for a week! *Bet Flis feels the same way,* was his last conscious thought.

A reminding whinny brought Jack wide awake and shivering. Great! Here he was practically naked, lying in the sand with the sun just maliciously nodding goodnight before disappearing over the closest hill. "They'll think something's happened to me,'' he muttered, shoving his legs and arms into his clothes, stuffing his socks in the saddle bag, and pulling his boots on over bare feet. Home was so close it wouldn't matter. At least his shorts were dry from sleeping in the sun.

"Come on, boy.'' Jack climbed into the saddle, flexing slightly stiff muscles that had seen more use today than they usually did. "Let's go home.'' He guided Old Prince back to the well-beaten path down to the river from the farm.

"OK, go for it," he called. It wouldn't take long on this smooth, straight stretch. The rhythmic cadence of hoofbeats lifted Jack's spirits.

The next instant, a short, sharp bark interrupted their progress. "Get out of the way, Dusty! Why'd they let you come, anyway?" Jack yelled at the dog only barely visible in the growing dusk.

Another bark. Old Prince spooked. With one quick rear of his forefeet that nearly unseated his rider, the horse swerved from the traveled path and plunged across the rolling hills toward stands of trees looming dark ahead.

Jack had all he could do to just hang on. Somehow in the unexpected incident he'd dropped the reins. Now he clung to the pommel, trying to talk sense into the frightened horse's head and vaguely hearing Dusty's barking gradually fade and die somewhere behind them.

C H A P T E R
10

A Night to Remember

Whoa, Old Prince. Stop, you dumb horse!'' Jack pressed his legs against the bay's sides and desperately held on. Lingering dusk gave way to gray gloom, but still, dodging trees and never decreasing the pace, they hurtled into the unknown. Several times Jack felt a low-hanging branch sweep his shoulder. He crouched as low in the saddle as he could get and still hang on, but still those reaching pine fingers seemed intent on snatching him off his horse. Minutes or hours or years later, Jack didn't know which, he felt Old Prince slowing. Then, a burst of pain shot through his head—and blackness.

He came to, not knowing where he was. Heavy breathing in his face, the creaking of leather, the smell of horse sweat, finally signaled to his aching head and brought him to a half-sitting position. Had he been hit by lightning? He tried to remember. A nose nuzzling against him and an apologetic neigh cleared his brain. Oh, yeah, Dusty had scared Old Prince, and sent him into a panic. Jack gingerly touched his head. Dampness on his fingers told him without his seeing it that he was bleeding.

Dizzy and a little sick, he reached for Old Prince's loose hanging reins. ''Thanks for not deserting me, old boy. But where are we?''

Another nicker didn't help. Now what? He shivered, suddenly chilly. How long had he been knocked out and lying on the needle-covered ground? The watch he didn't wear during chores would be a big help—if he had it. "Well I guess we'd better do something instead of just staying here." Speaking out loud did help. The sound of his voice and Old Prince's whinnied responses seemed to keep back the scariness of the night. In all the time Jack and Flis had been at the farm, they'd never ridden at night. The only times they'd been out after dark had been at church or school activities.

"How come there isn't a moon? That would help. I guess it isn't late enough for one, huh."

He touched his head again. It felt a little better, like it had quit bleeding. Jack managed to climb into the saddle. But before he did anything more than get a secure grip on the reins, he bowed his head. "God, I sure need Your help. It's too dark to find hoof prints. I don't have the foggiest idea of where home is. Help me, please."

He raised his head and peered into the darkness. Stars by the millions peeked down at him and cast a curious pattern of light and shadow, relieving the dead black. A feeling of control filled Jack and drove away some of his weakness. "It's up to me to get out of this. Come on, Old Prince, let's go." He neck-reined the bay and they started off to the right.

Old Prince picked his way under towering pines and across starlit open patches. Jack guided him toward the open as much as he could. The last thing he needed was another whack on the head. Five minutes later the horse stopped and neighed. Now what!

"Go on, boy," Jack urged.

Old Prince didn't budge.

"Go on, will you?" An aching head, empty stomach, and the weird black and silver night combined into irritation.

The bay still wouldn't budge.

"Great. Out in the middle of nowhere with a horse that balks and decides to stay here." Jack slid from the saddle, limped to his horse's head, then drew back in terror.

The ground just ahead fell away sharply into a sea of blackness. If

Old Prince had taken a few more steps, they'd have gone over into who knew what!

For a moment all Jack could do was cling to Old Prince's neck. Heart thudding, he carefully backed away, swung to the saddle, and turned the horse away from the precipice. Once back to safe ground he whispered, "Thanks, God." Then, "Thank you, Prince."

What should he do now? The feeling of being in control had vanished at the cliff's edge. There was no way he could find his way out of this predicament. His sudden laugh echoed from the canyon below him. Of all the times to get caught in a hopeless situation—not when he'd been asking for it by the way he acted but through no fault of his own.

"God," he cried into the night, "I know I haven't let You be in control the way I should. It's not too late, is it? I don't care about being P.K. the Great. I just want to get back to the farm where it's safe. You're going to have to help me. I don't know anything else to do, and I'm scared to try and pick another direction."

Only the rustle of leaves nearby answered.

Well, what had he expected? That God would shine a light down from heaven or miraculously turn Old Prince around?

"Please, God. I really need You—and not just for tonight, either."

A minute passed. Two. *Won't God do something, anything? What would Grandpa do if he got caught out like this?* Jack laughed again, this time bitterly. Grandpa knew every inch of land for miles around. He'd never get in such a mess.

From somewhere in Jack's brain pieces of a conversation started replaying. *"What if our horses run away and get lost?"* He could see Flis's wide-eyed expression.

"My horses are well-trained." He could see Grandpa, dead serious. Jack wrinkled his face trying to remember.

"Let them decide; they'll bring you safely home. Don't . . . make them go your way. Loosen their reins. Trust in their God-given instincts to take care of you."

Blood pumping through his veins, Jack pried his fingers from the reins, opening their death-grip. Old Prince immediately tossed his head and whinnied. Jack's fingers closed again. Did he dare trust the bay?

A new thought pounded at him. *Has God answered my prayer by helping me remember what Grandpa said?*

Again he forced his fingers open. "Let's go home, Old Prince," he called. His body tensed.

With a snort Old Prince pivoted and headed in the exact opposite direction from where Jack thought the farm lay. He pranced a bit, selected the ground he wanted to trod, and when he got into the open between clumps of trees, settled into a steady but slow pace. Once he veered sharply to the left, and his weary rider wondered if they'd come to the edge of another cliff. Then Jack saw a pile of big rocks blocking the way and sighed with relief.

The sound of gravel against Old Prince's hooves brought the boy to attention. The bay broke into a canter, and Jack noticed how much lighter the world had grown from the fat moon just climbing from behind a hill. "Hey, we're almost home!" All thought of pain and hunger and fear fled. He sat straighter in the saddle, actually enjoying the rush of the wind and wondered why he'd been so scared of the beautiful night world around him. Still the yellow light pouring from the farmhouse windows, Dusty's excited barking, Flis tearing out the front door and closely followed by Grandma and Grandpa, had never looked so good!

"Glad you're back, son." Powerful hands lifted him from the saddle. Strong arms held him close. "What happened?"

"Not now," Grandma interrupted. "Jack, get yourself inside, cleaned up, and back downstairs. You can tell us all about it after you eat."

Jack hugged his grandfather, but shook his head. "There's something I have to do first." He caught up Old Prince's reins and took a step toward the barn.

"I'll rub him down," Grandpa offered.

"No, sir. That's my job." Jack saw the wide smile cross Grandpa's face.

"Let me do it," Flis begged, her slender hands clasped together around Jack's arm.

"No, but thanks." He limped away, Old Prince trotting after him as though he hadn't run and walked and cantered for miles. It was all Jack's tired arms could do to curry the bay, but he made it. No way would he let anyone else care for his horse after what had happened. A final hug of the strong neck, a pat of the bay's nose, and he dropped the bolt of the barn door. Jack felt worn out, but satisfied.

Firelight glinted on Grandma's glasses, sparkled in Felicity's eyes, and shadowed Grandpa's face while Jack told his story. Warmed, filled with good food, the cut on his head dressed, Jack lay curled on the rug in front of the fire with Dusty next to him, "Just for tonight," as Grandpa said.

"I really didn't mean to be late," he told his little audience. He went on about falling asleep, racing home, Dusty spooking Old Prince, the wild rush ending with a branch knocking him from the saddle, awakening to a starlit night and strange surroundings, and having "a headache you wouldn't believe." When he got to the part about the horse saving them from pitching down a cliff, he saw Flis reach for a tissue. He hurried on.

"I knew then I couldn't do anything. God had to do it. I told Him I really needed His help and was sorry for the way I always want to control things. At first I wondered if He heard me because nothing happened, so I prayed again.

"Go on," Flis ordered when he stopped for breath.

Jack remembered those moments in the saddle and breathed hard. "I asked myself what Grandpa would do. Next thing I knew, I thought of what he'd said that time about trusting in his horses' God-given instincts and not trying to make them do what I thought they should." His fingers curled into fists and he relaxed them the way he'd done on the range. "All Old Prince needed was for me to let go." He stared into the dying embers of the fire. "I guess that's all God needed, too." He added, "Old Prince found the trail right away. I learned something else too. The only way to stay on the right trail is to let Jesus do the leading." He yawned mightily. "That's for me, for keeps." He yawned again, wondered if he'd dislocated his jaw, and stumbled to his feet. "If we're going to have worship, it had better be soon or I'll never make it!"

A NIGHT TO REMEMBER

"You bet we're having worship." Grandpa got out the Bible, read Jack's favorite Psalm—the 91st—then each of the four prayed, thanking God for taking care of Jack.

Jack had thought he'd sleep until noon but awoke at the usual time the next morning. The only trace left of his adventure was the scratched, swollen place on his forehead. He could hide it by brushing his hair a different way. Good. He didn't need anyone outside the family knowing how dumb he'd been.

He stared in the mirror. "Hold it, Nelson," he sternly told his image. "If you keep still about acting dumb by letting your horse run away, then no one will know how God saved you. Forget how you look and start speaking up about how neat God is!" It wouldn't be easy. Even though the Cottonwood kids accepted him now, they weren't all that much into religion. It wouldn't be all that easy going back to Vancouver Academy next fall, either, facing all the kids he used to try to boss.

Some of his feelings dampened his enthusiasm for the perfect June day. Besides, something puzzled him. At breakfast he asked, "Uh, didn't you go out looking for me when it started to get dark?"

"I wanted to." Flis sent an unreadable look at Grandpa.

He just smiled and buttered another hot biscuit. "I gave you until 10 o'clock to get back. You got here a little after nine."

"By 10?" Jack curiously let jam drip off his knife and waited for the answer.

"If you hadn't become frightened enough by then to let God take care of you and use your own common sense in trusting Old Prince to bring you home, it meant you'd been hurt." Something in his eyes silenced the dozen questions Jack had been going to ask.

A few days later Jack dug in the bottom of his suitcase for a shirt he had tossed in but hadn't needed until now. Farm work could be hard on clothes. Some of the shirts he wore for chores showed it. "What . . .?" A crumpled, hand-written page fell out of the folds, "Musta dropped in when I packed," Jack muttered and unfolded it. His face turned scarlet. After he read it, he tore it into tiny bits and hid them in the bottom of the garbage can. Then he locked his door and knelt by his bed.

"God, about that letter—I'm sorry. I can't believe I whined like that. It sounds just like Dusty when he was a puppy, always sneaking around doing dumb stuff. Uh, thanks for letting me be here and for keeping on sending people and a horse to save me when I needed it. Things are gonna be a whole lot different after this, I promise." He thought of his temper, his struggles. "Even though it won't be easy, I know You'll forgive me, and help me keep on trying. Amen." He got up feeling both small and big.

When the school semester that Jack and Flis had dreaded ended, they reluctantly told the other kids goodbye. "No, we won't be back next year," Jack said, "but we're sure glad we could finish this year, and we won't forget Cottonwood High School. Maybe we can even come down some weekend next year during basketball season."

"You'd better." Karen grinned the uptilted grin that always left Jack feeling great.

"Yeah." Dick punched his friend's arm. "And don't forget to tell—I mean ask—your folks if we can come up for a weekend."

"I won't. You're two of the best friends we've ever had." Jack walked away quickly. No use getting sticky.

A week later a familiar Toyota pulled into the yard. Nelsons erupted from the car, the house, and the barn. "Hey, look, *Dad's* driving!" Jack stared in amazement at the tall, deeply tanned man smiling at them all.

"Dad, you're really well!" Only Jack caught the poignant relief in his sister's voice. Flis threw herself against Dad. Bright tears shone. She hugged him hard.

"You two don't look any the worse for farm life," Mom said as she inspected them.

"Why didn't you tell us you were coming?"

"Grandma always gets ready for company like an army planned to invade when she knows people are coming," Dad teased. "We got in early yesterday afternoon, found an empty but spotless house, and here we are." His dark eyes told the rest of the story. "We've missed you."

"How long can you stay?" Grandma wanted to know.

Jack could see her mind already turning with who'd sleep where, what to make for meals, and stuff.

"We should get right back." Dad grinned at Mom. " But we aren't going to. If it's OK with you, we'd like to stick around a few days. One of the things the doctor told me is to start doing what we want to do sometimes instead of just what we think we have to and should do. Not just me," he broke off quickly. "Anyone. Too many people never get around to being good enough to themselves."

"I'll say amen to that." Mom put her arm through Dad's and looked up at him. The love in her face made Jack grin.

"You two act like a couple on a honeymoon," he accused.

"Second honeymoon. Next time, though, we want our kids with us."

"We'll buy that, huh, Flis?" She nodded and Jack said, "Get into some old clothes, will you? Grandpa and I have work to do and can't let dudes from the city slow us down."

Busy days, peaceful afternoons, and quiet evenings gobbled up the visit. Finally, Jack handed Felix to Flis to hold, ordered Dusty into the car, and told Dad and Mom, "That's everything." But before he climbed in, he hugged Grandma, then Grandpa. "Thanks—for everything," he whispered. He cleared his throat. "Uh—I love you, both."

"Us too." Grandpa didn't bother to correct the poor grammar, and Jack fully understood. "Remember, any time you can come—" he waved at the neat gardens, fields, and rolling hills with cattle and horses, and his eyes twinkled. "Always plenty of work for another good hand."

"Thanks. I won't forget." Jack started to the car, but Grandpa said in a low voice, "Soon as you get home, you might want to measure yourself."

"OK. Bye." The Toyota swung into the road. Grandma and Grandpa and the farm got smaller and smaller and finally disappeared behind a hill.

"Do you feel kind of let down?" Jack whispered to Flis. He wouldn't let their folks hear for the world. "I mean, it's like going back to outer space or coming from outer space or something."

"I know." She automatically stroked Felix. "The animals aren't going to be the only ones with some adjusting to do." She fell silent and Jack did, too. Somehow he needed the time and space to build a bridge between two such different ways of life.

"It looks just the same!" Flis exclaimed when they pulled into the drive.

"Whadya expect? That it would be painted purple?" But Jack scrambled out of the car even faster than she did. He unlocked the door to the quiet kitchen, comparing it with Grandma's old-fashioned kitchen, then walked through, glad for the feeling of "homeyness" that filled him, but also a little sad at how much he missed the big farm house. When he came to his room, he quickly checked it out. Everything was the way he'd left it. Then why did it seem unfamiliar? It hadn't changed. *But I have. I could have died, a couple of times. I'm not the same Jack. I'll be 15 in a few more days. Grandpa said to get measured.*

Jack flattened a ruler across the top of his head and pencil-marked the wall. He rubbed his eyes and stared again, then carefully erased the new mark.

"Flis? Come here a minute, will you?"

"I'm unpacking. What do you want?"

"Just come here—please?"

She stuck her tousled head in the door, and Jack asked, "Measure me, will you?"

She rolled her eyes the way she used to do but grabbed the ruler. "OK. Stand straight!" She marked the wall. "Slide out." He did. "Jack, look!" she screamed.

The new mark clearly showed a whole inch above the top mark made the previous December.

"What's going on in here?" Dad and Mom walked in.

"Jack grew a whole inch!"

Dad looked at Mom, then Flis, then Jack. "I'm not surprised." Jack knew a silly grin must be spreading over his face, but he didn't even care. Especially when Dad said, "Be sure and let Grandpa know."

"I will—right now." Jack dug an unused postcard from his suitcase, scribbled a few words, and ran out to the mail box.

A few days later an answer came in Grandpa's strong handwriting. Jack laughed when he read, "Not just an inch, praise God. Not just an inch," then tucked it in his Bible so he wouldn't forget.